Praise for

Angels, Dragons
& Vultures

"*Raising investment for your business can be a tricky task. Simon's book* Angels, Dragons and Vultures *charts the challenges in a down-to-earth, readable and often humorous way. If you are looking to expand your business or planning to set one up, this is well worth a read.*"

Richard Branson

"*A helpful, expert and practical guide for those risking the world of venture capital funding. Full of excellent advice.*"

Tim Waterstone

"*Simon Acland has written an insider's guide to the opaque and much sought-after world of venture capital.* Angels, Dragons and Vultures *decodes the industry and offers sound advice for those who will engage with it.*"

Julie Meyer, founder of Entrepreneur Country, CEO of Ariadne Capital, and a Dragon on the BBC's Dragon's Den Online

Angels,
Dragons
&
Vultures

To Nadia
with best wishes

Simon

15. ii . 2014

For all the entrepreneurs with whom I have had
the privilege to work

Angels, Dragons & Vultures

How to tame your investors...

and *not* lose your company

Simon Acland

NICHOLAS BREALEY
PUBLISHING

First published by
Nicholas Brealey Publishing in 2011

3–5 Spafield Street
Clerkenwell, London
EC1R 4QB, UK
Tel: +44 (0)20 7239 0360
Fax: +44 (0)20 7239 0370

20 Park Plaza, Suite 1115A
Boston
MA 02116, USA
Tel: (888) BREALEY
Fax: (617) 523 3708

www.nicholasbrealey.com
www.venture-capital-advice.com

© Simon Acland 2011
The right of Simon Acland to be identified as the author of this work has been
asserted in accordance with the Copyright, Designs and Patents Act 1988.

Library of Congress Cataloging-in-Publication Data

Acland, Simon.
  Angels, dragons & vultures : how to tame your investors-- and not lose
your company / Simon Acland.
    p. cm.
  Includes index.
  ISBN 978-1-85788-551-4
  1. Venture capital. I. Title. II. Title: Angels, dragons and vultures.
  HG4751.A25 2011
  658.15'224--dc22

2010036885

ISBN 978-1-85788-551-4

British Library Cataloguing in Publication Data
A catalogue record for this book is available from the
British Library.

Printed in Finland by WS Bookwell.

Contents

The Venture Capital Bestiary

Angels, Dragons, Vultures: what are these beasts? Angels sound nice; Dragons and Vultures rather less so. But then Angels can be satanic. Dragons are sometimes friendly. And Vultures come in handy for disposing of corpses and clearing up rubbish.

In the context of this book, Angels invest their own money as venture capital in a business.

Vultures also make venture capital investments, but with other people's money. That way Vultures hope to earn enough to become as rich as an Angel.

And Dragons? Well, they're Angels with such a thirst for publicity that they can't resist breathing fire on television.

Angels can be Dragons, but Dragons are always Angels. Angels are sometimes Vultures, or have been in the past. Vultures can be Angels or even Dragons, or they want to be, and get called all sorts of other, even less flattering names as well. And just to complicate matters further, in the US Dragons are not Dragons at all, nor do they have a den. Instead, they are Sharks and they live in a tank.

Is that as clear as mud?

WHAT SORT OF BEAST SHOULD YOU BE TO READ THIS BOOK?

I hope that the book may be of some interest to Angels, Dragons, and Vultures, but it is written for the beasts without whom Angels, Dragons, and Vultures would be unable to exist – entrepreneurs.

My talk of Dragons and Vultures runs the risk of character-izing the entrepreneur as their helpless prey, some poor species of defenseless ungulate with little chance of escape. But the entrepreneur is really the king of this particular jungle, the Lion. Without the entrepreneur, Angels, Dragons, and Vultures would have no purpose. On their own they cannot exist.

So first and foremost this is a book for entrepreneurs, and it is dedicated to the entrepreneurs with whom I have been privileged to work during the course of my career. They are Lions because of the bravery and energy it takes to set up a business or to step into a risky venture, because of their hunger, and because of their style.

A WORD OF WARNING

There is one sobering fact I must lay out for the Lions before I go any further.

During my venture capital career I sat on the board of 23 companies. In only 7 cases – less than one third – was the chief executive I originally backed still in that position at the end.

An even more surprising statistic is that in 4 out of 7 of these cases, the company concerned had gone bust. Over half of the instances where the chief executive remained unchanged resulted in failure. Yet in total, only 5 out of the 23 companies I backed went bust – including those where the chief executive remained unchanged. In one instance the CEO was changed and the company still went bust. In only 3 out of 18 successful cases was the original CEO still in place.

Is it fair to draw the conclusion that to achieve a venture capital success, especially from early-stage investment, it is nearly always necessary for the chief executive to change as the company grows and develops? My personal portfolio is a small sample, I know, but that is the conclusion toward which I would be forced based on my direct experience.

The table opposite shows the picture starkly. Overall my failure rate was 22%; not too bad for an early-stage investor. But

Company outcome	CEO changed	%	CEO unchanged	%	Total	%
Survivors	15	94	2	43	18	78
Failures	1	6	4	57	5	22
Total	16	100	7	100	23	100

when the founding CEO remained in place to the bitter end, there was a bitter end in 57% of cases. When a change took place, the failure rate fell to a remarkable 6%.

If until a moment ago you were an entrepreneur who was considering raising venture capital – a Lion who was summoning the courage to expose him- or herself to the spells, claws, and talons of Angels, Dragons, or Vultures – you may now be closing this book and putting it back on the shelf, deciding not to buy it or go further with your plan. If you are a founding chief executive who already has outside investors, you may be cursing under your breath and doing just the same. But please wait a moment. Keep reading for another line or two.

Written from the perspective of a venture capitalist, this book draws on a career's worth of experience of mistakes made by entrepreneurs – some of their own making, and some into which they were cajoled by their investors. By sharing the lessons of these mistakes, I hope that I will help you toward an outcome for yourself that is both lucrative and emotionally satisfactory. I hope that this book will help put *you* into the top box of the middle column in the table above.

ANOTHER DEFINITION

This is not a book about private equity. "Venture capital" and "private equity" are terms that are far too often interchanged and confused. They are as different as pride and prejudice, or sense and sensibility.

Venture capital means investment in a business which needs equity funding to grow, normally because it cannot generate enough cash itself from its existing trading activities to fulfill its plans. Perhaps the investment is to be used pre-revenue – so before the company is generating any cash at all – to research or develop a product or a technology. One way or another, venture capital is often used to allow a company the dangerous luxury of making losses. By definition, therefore, venture capital carries a high element of inherent risk and needs to offer to its provider the potential of a reward high enough to balance that risk.

Before its first venture capital investment – from Angel, Dragon, or Vulture – a company will typically be wholly owned by its founders and management team. Generally businesses that raise venture capital are quite young, at an early stage in their development. If a company raises venture capital after being around for a while, it may be about to make a step change, perhaps moving from providing a service to selling a product, or grafting a new activity onto an existing, related rootstock. Usually all, and certainly most, of the new capital will be invested in the business, not paid out to existing or former owners.

Private equity is quite different. It typically involves buying an established business from its owners. This can be a management buy-out – an MBO – by the existing team, often from a corporate owner. Or it can be a management buy-in – an MBI – with a new team acquiring an existing business. A BIMBO sounds much more fun but, disappointingly, as a buy-in management buy-out, it is simply a hybrid of the two. In any event, with these structures all or most of the money goes outside the business to pay off previous shareholders. Most businesses backed by private equity are profitable and cash generative. They are often geared up with significant levels of borrowing to provide better returns on the equity investment, and the cash flow from the business is used to service and repay the debt. It follows, therefore, that they are usually well established, and inherently lower risk than businesses backed by venture capital. Often a large element of the risk associated with private equity investment is caused by the financing structure. Private equity failures mainly result when the debt element of a deal is too large and servicing it places an unbearable burden on the business. The debris left in the private equity world by the 2008 credit crunch and subsequent recession shows this very clearly.

A few of the points made in this book may be relevant to these private equity deals – especially around how to build, maintain, and manage your relationship with your backers – but in most cases they are too large and late stage to have much in common with real venture capital. They have a very different dynamic. Just as importantly, a different type of person is normally involved, both on the side of the investor and on the side of the management team.

There, I have used that phrase already. I have implied that there are two sides, two opposing teams, in a venture capital deal. That, of course, is one of the main problems. It is perhaps the main reason why in my career I have seen as many companies destroyed by venture capital as made by it. This book is about how to keep the Lions, Angels, Dragons, and Vultures all on the same side.

Some of my comments may appear uncomplimentary, even hostile, to venture capital practitioners. This is not my intention. In fact I am being thoroughly unfair in using the term Vulture generically for a professional venture capitalist. Really Vulture should only be used for a particular type of aggressive, opportunistic investor. So please forgive me my sense of humor. I do not want to be lynched the next time I go to Menlo Park or Mayfair.

I have many good friends in the venture capital industry, and bear for them both respect and affection. I had a lot of fun during my career, and managed to make a bit of money. It is an exciting, varied, and challenging job. The industry performs a valuable economic function. I hope that by advising entrepreneurs on how to take well-informed decisions, this book will help, not hinder, my former colleagues.

A NOTE ABOUT GENDER

Politically incorrect it may be, but in this book I am old-fashioned and stick to "he" and "him" rather than "he or she," "him or her," and so on. This is not because I think women cannot or should not run businesses – in fact my wife is a chief executive and does it far better than I ever could – but just because it makes for an easier prose style.

Having said that, I will share one more statistic about my time as a Vulture which I always regretted and have never been able to explain: not one of the businesses that I personally backed was run by a woman, and in the whole history of my firm we backed female chief executives just twice. One was very successful and one was not.

The only possible explanation I have been able to think of is that women are too sensible, too creative, too intelligent, and too inventive to need to raise venture capital for their businesses. They develop them in different ways. That brings me neatly on to my first chapter.

CHAPTER ONE

Venture Capital: Do You Really Want It?

*Can you trust doctors who don't take
their own medicine?*

You may well think that is a strange question to ask at the beginning of a book about venture capital. You may be so sure that venture capital will be your ticket to fortune and fame that you can afford to skip this chapter. I certainly don't want to put you off. But I do want to make sure that you go into this with your eyes wide open – not with your eyes wide shut.

Very few venture capital firms have outside shareholders. Most are fiercely jealous of their own independence. Those that start with outside investors often buy out those shareholders to regain total control just as soon as they can – and celebrate wildly when they have done so. And many venture firms suffer from succession problems precisely because their founders or senior partners are so jealous of their equity that young up-and-coming members of their team are not cut into the action soon enough – or at all. Nobody understands the value of hanging onto their own equity like a venture capitalist. They extol to entrepreneurs all the benefits an equity investment can bring, but they are not so good at swallowing their own medicine.

"It is far better to have a small slice of a big cake," they say, "than to have a large slice of a small one." But most of them are extremely reluctant to sell any portion of their own cake. No group – except perhaps the television evangelists of the Deep Southern states – is so good at not practicing what it fervently preaches.

Consider the fact that venture firms which are owned by other financial institutions are known in their industry as "captives." That word encapsulates venture capitalists' attitude to having outside shareholders in their own business. Pause. Think. Do you really want to become a "captive" of your venture capital investor?

One of the main motivations for many entrepreneurs is independence. Remember why you set your business up in the first place. Your desire to have control over your own destiny must have been an important reason. A considerable part of the reason you stepped out of the relative security of a salaried job in someone else's company may have been in order to be your own master.

So before you sell equity in your business to any outside investor, whether Angel, Dragon, or Vulture, search your heart. Be sure that you really are willing to relinquish some control. Selling even a minority stake means that you will lose your independence. You may still technically exercise control through a majority shareholding, but you will have to take into account the views of others in the way you run your business. Their economic interests will have to be considered. As a director of your company you will have an obligation – both moral and legal – to consider your outside shareholders' needs and interests.

It will no longer be totally your business. You will find yourself operating under a new set of rules, and those rules will not be entirely of your own making. Your company's constitution will be governed by a new Certificate of Incorporation, an Investor Rights Agreement, and a string of other documents in North America, or by a complex Shareholders' Agreement and weighty new Articles of Association in the UK, and similar contracts in other jurisdictions. (See Chapter 5 for chapter and verse on those special instruments of torture.) Those documents will give your minority shareholders entrenched rights which to an extent negate your ability to exercise control of your company through your shareholding.

And if the expansionary plan on which you have been encouraged to embark does not bear fruit, or if the fruit takes too long to ripen and the money in the bank runs down, you may find yourself completely at the mercy of the only person sitting at your boardroom table with cash to invest – your venture capital beast. (See Chapter 6 for more on this.)

Once you have brought an outside shareholder into your business, you cannot step backward in time and undo what you have done. Very occasionally an entrepreneur manages to pull off the trick of buying back his own business at a lower value than the price he sold it for. In my personal sample of 23 deals, it happened just once. On the few occasions when it does occur, it normally means that the business has not succeeded anyway. It is much more common that the first round of investment leads to a second round, and then maybe a third. (Chapter 11 covers the perils of these "follow-on" rounds of funding.) That first 30% stake you sold becomes 55% and then you are no longer even the majority shareholder. Then something goes wrong, and your investors lose confidence in you and tighten the thumbscrews. And then you find you are no longer a shareholder at all. Or a director. Or an employee. You have lost your company, your job, and your chance of wealth and fame.

If things go well, those disappointments may not happen. But in any event, by taking outside investment you have made a commitment to your venture capital beast. It will probably be specifically stated in that Stock Purchase or Shareholders' Agreement of yours, but even if it is not, the practical and moral commitment is there. You will have to provide your Vulture, your Angel, or your Dragon with an exit. (I cover the intricacies of exits in Chapter 12.) Suffice it to say at this point that you are committing yourself to a path which should lead to the sale of your business, or to the achievement of a public market in its shares. Your outside shareholders are investing on the basis that you will provide them with the opportunity to sell their shares via one of these routes within a timescale that makes sense for themselves and their own investors. That is part of the bargain you are striking with them and they will have every right to be aggrieved if you renege on it. You will no longer be able to run your company as a "lifestyle business," living off what you can make and adjusting your input to it according to the way you wish to run your life.

ALTERNATIVES

So before you take the plunge, examine carefully whether this is really what you want. Also examine whether you really *have* to raise equity capital. Is there absolutely no other way of achieving your objectives? Whether or not there is an alternative may depend on the nature of your business and your personal position. It will also depend on your own appetite for risk.

Typical studies (for example one conducted by Cambridge Business Research in 2009, "The role of micro funds in the financing of new technology-based firms") show that around 50% of businesses resort to credit card funding. A similar number use bank overdrafts, almost inevitably guaranteed by the business's proprietor or secured on their property. Perhaps a quarter use other commercial loans and hire purchase or leasing; 5% secure grant funding; and somewhere between 1% and 3% raise external equity capital. So only a very small minority of businesses resort to Angels, Dragons, or Vultures.

Now, of course, many of the businesses covered in these studies raise small sums of money. Most of them are not suitable for venture capital treatment in any case. Many have no possibility or ambition to be anything other than a lifestyle business. But even for those that are suitable subjects for a Vulture, Angel, or Dragon, it may be a wise move to use small amounts of funding from these alternative sources to get as far down the track as possible before raising outside capital.

A phrase I particularly dislike, which is often used in early-stage equity investing circles, is the 3Fs. This stands for

"Friends, Family, and Fools." It may be foolish to invest in an early-stage business if you do not understand what you are getting yourself into. It is certainly foolish to invest money that you cannot afford to lose. But to describe in this way individuals who might provide early-stage funding partly out of generosity and optimism is churlish in the extreme. It also reflects badly on the entrepreneur who takes money for his business on this basis. If foolish friends or family invest in your business to get it started, you should treat them in the same way as any other outside shareholder or lender, and do your utmost to make sure that they get a fair return on their investment. Otherwise you may find yourself alone in the corner, and rightly so, at the next family wedding. Or simply not invited. It may be easier and less formal to raise money from them than from a professional Angel, Dragon, or Vulture, but the rules and obligations that you should impose on yourself should be no different.

THE 3CS

Let me coin a new phrase that I prefer: the 3Cs. This stands for "Colleagues, Customers, and Collaborators."

"Colleagues" is clear enough. Getting a friend, or a family member, to put money into your company so that you have to draw your own belt less tight is one thing. Having a colleague, who shares your ambitions and objectives, tighten his or her belt to the same notch as yours is quite another. Starting a business can be a lonely activity. That, of course, is the very reason some people do it; others find it easier to spread the load. Later on, perhaps, you may find that the load is not as evenly distributed as it once was (I cover that eventuality in Chapter 10), but at least it can be a fair way to start out.

"Customers" is pretty clear, too, although you don't have any and your product is little more than an idea. But can't you pre-sell your idea to a customer? You may have to offer advantageous terms, and perhaps compromise on some intellectual property rights for a specific sector or for a certain period. Nevertheless, at least work through whether offering an early customer a sweet deal is a better option for you than selling part of your equity to an investor irrevocably, for once and for all. Your customer will certainly demand less control than your investor.

Perhaps you are worried that development for a specific customer will lead to product compromises. Maybe you think that a customer-specific design will have no application in the wider market. More often than not, in fact, it is the other way round. The venture capital-funded generic product is often developed in too much of a vacuum, so that it meets theoretical customers' needs but does not give them what they actually want. Working with an early customer on a co-development can be the best way of making sure that the product is something that the market wants to buy. So starting a business off in this way may not only obviate the need to sell too much equity too early, it can actually help you to build a better business.

Microsoft, the most successful software company of all time, did not raise a cent in venture capital until 1981, when it was six years old. Bootstrap Bill is not only a character from *Pirates of the Caribbean*. At the very beginning, in 1975, Bill Gates wrote to MITS – which had just launched the Altair 8800, perhaps the first true personal computer – and offered to write a BASIC language for it. Gates and Paul Allen continued to build products for people who paid them to do so; in other words, they carried out development projects. They did not formulate a vision of the product the world needed and lose money developing it. They found a customer who needed a product, who often had an idea of the product they needed because they already had customers of their own, and developed their product for them. Even MS-DOS, the operating system that took Microsoft into the big time, was developed under contract to

IBM for the IBM PC. Part of Gates's genius lay in striking the commercial terms around these development contracts, which in the case of MS-DOS enabled him to keep the intellectual property rights so that he could sell the same operating system to other PC manufacturers.

Apple is another famous name that started with customer funding. In 1976, Steve Wozniak, the brilliant engineer who founded Apple with Steve Jobs, designed and built the Apple I before raising any outside capital. He was still working at Hewlett-Packard. Jobs took an order for 100 units worth $50,000 from the Byte Shop. They funded this order by buying the parts for the computers on credit, and getting the Byte Shop to pay in cash. It was not until the iconic Apple II was designed that the first outside angel funding was invested to manufacture the product in early 1977, and not until 1978 that the first institutional venture capital round took place. When Apple floated in 1981, it was the largest initial public offering since the Ford Motor Company in 1956.

If winning a development contract is not an option for you, can you fund your product development through consultancy? Can you eke out your cash by drawing a smaller salary – or no salary at all – or by cutting other corners? And of course, the further you can take your business under its own steam, the more certain you will be of the market opportunity. Yahoo!, which in the mid to late 1990s reigned supreme as the dominant internet portal, started in 1994 as a collection of links to research papers created for their personal use by two graduate students at Stanford, Jerry Yang and David Filo. Other students heard about it and began sending in links themselves, asking for them to be added. It was only once the momentum had led to a proven demand that Yahoo! was set up as a business.

As certainty and market validation increase, the better the terms become when you do raise that first tranche of outside capital, and the easier that is to achieve. The risks will have reduced, and the potential rewards will have increased, making the equation much more attractive for the investor. This is especially difficult in the case of deep science-based businesses, where a large amount of capital will be required. These businesses should choose very carefully the moment they emerge into the commercial world, breaking out of an academic cocoon, for example, or spinning out of a larger business. Venture capital equity funding is often best used for commercializing a technology and turning it into a real product, not for developing the technology itself. If investors are called on to take the strain too early, too much money will be consumed; even with a positive outcome, the amount invested may exceed the business's eventual value. If it is tough for investors to make money, it will be just as tough, or tougher, for the inventor or entrepreneur.

THE THREE LAWS OF ROBOTICS

This is the first of several anecdotes based on events from my career that I use in various places to illustrate my points. For reasons of confidentiality I use a fictional style and omit names; I assure you that the stories are genuine. Here are two which illustrate alternative ways of getting your business off the ground.

Both men looked as if they should be smoking pipes. One sat at the laboratory desk; the other paced up and down, gesticulating anxiously.

"Yes, we could develop the control system you want. But it would divert us from the direction I want to go. The market we want to focus on is machine tool controllers, not industrial robots. I've got the core technology, and know what needs to be done, but it is just not our real priority. We'd need to build a new team and write a lot of special code, even a new programming language."

The man at the desk shifted uncomfortably from side to side as if his rough tweed jacket was too thick for the pleasant autumn day. "What if we were to place a development contract with you? On a 'cost plus' basis, of course. We'd have paid for the work, so we would have to own the IP, naturally…"

The pacing professor stopped in his tracks, a disconcerted expression spreading across his round face.

"…exclusively in its application to industrial robots. You could reuse the technology for other applications – your precious machine tools, for example. You could even have a go at an automated guided vehicle. Then you'd have all the components of an FMS. Sorry, flexible manufacturing system – I know you hate acronyms."

The professor started walking again, but rather slowly, as if deep in thought. "Mmm. It is a big commitment. It would probably take three years. So we'd have to have some decent royalties on the robots you sold at the end of the program. 2%? Running for 10 years? Then there's the value of what we've already built. You would have to make an up-front payment for the license."

The up-front payment, and the profits on the development contract, eliminated the need to raise venture capital in the first year. Far from selling the company's technology birthright, the development contract formed a cornerstone of the business plan when it was later decided to raise venture capital to accelerate growth in sectors outside robotics. The development contract also provided potential investors with a valuable endorsement of the company's technology.

THE RIGHT CALL?

"I just don't see how we can make ends meet if we leave."

The older man's eyes were worried behind his glasses as he ruffled his thinning hair. His youngest colleague, full of cocky energy, bounced on the balls of his feet. The other two watched pensively.

"We know they'll pay £850 per day for skilled network planners. The four of us'd get more, £1,000 or even £1,250. We already know most of the people we'd hire, and all in we wouldn't even have to pay them half that. We might have to drop our salaries a bit from what we are used to, but that should give us enough to bring in a couple of guys just to work on product development. Then, as the tool's functionality grows, we'll be able to charge more and do the network planning quicker."

"And I could get to work on the service node platform concept. If we get the architecture right, we won't have to think too much about the detailed application before we find our first customer. We could probably get them to pay us to write the first application – and that might be the best one to sell to the rest of the industry."

By the time they decided to raise venture capital, they had built a revenue stream from consultancy and product development of over £4 million. This attracted the interest of investors, reduced the amount of capital required, and increased the valuation at which capital was raised.

The service node platform was used to build a pre-paid cellphone billing system for one particular customer. The intellectual property was retained. The demand for the product, indicated by the first customer, was soon confirmed by interest from other phone operators. It rapidly became the company's main product line.

Although the strategic focus was on driving the software products into international markets, and particularly on exploiting the prepaid billing platform, the consultancy business was maintained and generated valuable cash flow. The business grew fast, and a second round of venture capital took place at a much higher valuation.

When, two and a half years after the first venture capital round, the company was sold to a major international software group for £50 million, the management team and senior staff still held a significant majority of the equity.

WINDOWS OF OPPORTUNITY

Sometimes the decision to raise venture capital is driven by the concern that a window of opportunity is about to close. If you do not raise enough capital to exploit it, somebody else will establish an unassailable position in the market you wanted for yourself. Occasionally this may be correct, but in my experience, more often windows of opportunity tend both to open and to close more slowly than you might expect. More of the businesses with which I have been involved have made the mistake of developing their product too early than too late. Consumers tend to take longer than entrepreneurs expect to change the way they lead their lives. Enterprises take even longer to change the way they do business. It is understandable – the entrepreneur's light bulb switches on, he has a great idea, he comes up with a new way of doing something that's miles better, cheaper, quicker, more elegant, and more fun and he thinks everyone will want it yesterday – but it doesn't happen like that.

Google wasn't the first web search company. Apple didn't invent the digital download of music. Microsoft wasn't the first company to develop a windows-based operating system. They all carefully watched others spending money to develop a market. They saw the mistakes these pioneers made, either technological, or marketing, or both, and developed better ways of doing the same. Then they came into the market and plucked the fruit when it was plump and ripe.

If your business depends only on being somewhere first for its competitive advantage, if market occupancy is your sole rampart against incoming competition, then frankly you are not likely to have much of a business. Cynical Vultures, their feathers ruffled by the bursting of the technology bubble in 2000, quickly renamed first-mover advantage "first-mover disadvantage."

IT ISN'T JUST ABOUT THE MONEY...

Ah. I knew you were a modest, self-perceptive individual. You understand your strengths and weaknesses. You know that your experience is not all-encompassing. There are aspects of running a business that you still have to learn. You don't just want money; you also want *help* from your investor.

Vultures are good at telling the world what they can do to help the businesses they back. Angels are more modest, quietly confident in their abilities and experience. Dragons – well, Dragons are perhaps even louder than Vultures in talking up their abilities, but then they are more likely to have built businesses themselves. In Chapter 6 I talk about what added value you can realistically expect from your venture capital beast.

There is nothing wrong with seeking added value from your investment partner. Recognizing your own limitations is as important in business as it is in life. But remember what it says about you to your beast. You are effectively saying that you might not have all the skills as CEO to take your company through to exit.

That is fine, of course, so long as you recognize at the beginning that in order to achieve your share of success you might have to be one of the 16 in the table I showed you in the Introduction. If the prospect of handing over the reins of your company is too horrible to contemplate, then start off self-funding on a less ambitious trajectory. Fill in the gaps in your skills with practical experience, and only raise outside capital when you are confident that you know it all. And good luck to you.

...BUT MONEY IS STILL IMPORTANT

Although business isn't just about money, money is a very important part of it. And one of the most basic business principles is that over a period of time you need to bring in more money than you lay out. In many businesses that is measured from day to day or week to week; some may have more leeway and be able to sustain a loss-making, or cash-negative, month, quarter, or even year.

Raising dollops of equity investment creates the opportunity to make losses, or to be cash negative, for as long as the investment lasts. Sometimes this makes good business sense. Two, three, even five or more years of loss-making product investment can lead to a gloriously profitable, cash-generative future, where profits far exceed the previous losses, or at least where the value of the business or the technology that has been created outweighs the sums invested.

However, it can also mean that you lose good business disciplines. You become addicted to the venture capital drug. Another fix becomes the easy option. (In Chapter 8 I talk about the need at some point to wean yourself off the venture capital addiction.)

So before you stick the needle in for the first time, make sure this really is what you want to do.

CHAPTER TWO

Understanding Venture Capital Beasts

Don't use a long spoon to sup with the devil.
Do get close to him and watch how he eats.

So you have looked at your business from every angle. You can see the opportunity to build it into something substantial. The market is there. Your product is almost ready and it will definitely meet the market need. You have thought hard about the ominous warnings of Chapter 1, but you cannot see any means to seize the opportunity without investment way beyond your own financial resources. No alternative remains: you will have to play Faust.

You understand intimately the inner workings of your own company. You have carefully modeled the business that you hope it will become. But have you looked equally carefully at the business models of the investors from whom you hope to raise money – the Mephistopheles to whom you will have to sell your soul?

I make no apology for going on at some length in this chapter about the venture capital model. After all, before you approach investors for funding you need to understand what they are looking for; and after you have taken their money you need to understand the pressures on them and the behavior that those pressures may drive.

THE VULTURES

Most venture capital firms are small businesses; far smaller, in fact, than the ambitions of the companies they back. They can seem powerful organizations because they appear to have access to money, and because they often occupy flashy offices in expensive locations. But appearances can be deceptive. Before you start approaching investors, pause to consider the economics that drive venture capital firms.

Fees

The main source of income for a venture capital firm is the management fee it receives from the institutions or individuals who invest in its funds. Although there has been some downward pressure toward 2%, the industry standard is still generally 2.5% per annum, normally paid quarterly. A simple rule of thumb, therefore, is that a firm with $20 million under management will have revenue of $500,000; a firm with $50 million under management, revenue of $1.25 million; one with $100 million, revenue of $2.5 million; and so on. Before you approach a venture firm for funding, find out how much capital they have under management and how many staff they employ, and you will be able to gain a quick idea of how comfortable they are – whether they have achieved "critical mass," or whether they are still having to scrabble around and earn money in other ways in order to make ends meet.

A few firms have delighted their investors by adopting "budget-based" fees, where they agree to draw a management fee which covers an agreed level of overhead, rather than a fee directly related to funds under management. These are very much the exception, however. And call me cynical, but budget-based fees are generally adopted only by firms which have done so well that they hardly need to earn money any more, or where their success justifies a very generous level of budgeted salary.

Of course, there are subtle variations on the fee model according to how a fund is structured. A venture capital fund raised from institutional investors – pension funds, endowments, insurance companies, banks, and the like – will

21

normally be structured as a limited partnership. This is the industry standard in the US, Europe, and Asia.

This type of fund is drawn down from investors – the limited partners, or LPs for short – in tranches as each underlying investment is made. The objective of this "just-in-time" drawdown structure is to maximize the internal rate of return on the fund. This IRR, essentially a compound annual return, is the most important yardstick by which the manager – the general partner (yes, you've guessed it, GP for short) – will be measured when the time comes for them to raise the next fund. Even though not all the money is invested in the fund up front, the management fee is calculated with reference to the total amount of money committed by the investors.

Limited partnership venture capital funds typically have a fixed-term life of ten years, with an option to extend for two further years and perhaps beyond in case some of the investments remain unrealized by then. For the primary investment period of the fund, the management fee is usually fixed, whether the value of the fund goes up or down. Normally, as it happens, the value of the fund goes down in the early years, because failures appear first and it takes longer to build a business to success than for it to go bust. In the industry jargon, "lemons ripen earlier than plums." One might conclude from this statement that few Vultures have ever grown citrus fruit; in fact, as you and I know, lemon trees flower and fruit simultaneously all year round.

The graphical effect to which this mantra gives rise is known as the "J curve." In the early years of a fund, valuations usually fall below cost, before beginning to rise again (one hopes) as successes emerge. GPs and LPs hope that about halfway through the fund's life, perhaps sooner, the valuation curve will cross the X axis again, and rise steeply in the later years as a result of the big winners. So in model funds, the graph you get if you plot the value of a fund against time is shaped like a J.

The point of the commitment-linked fee structure for fund investors (the limited partners) is that they want to be sure that the venture firm to which they have entrusted their money is stable and will have enough revenue to cover the costs of effectively managing the fund and its underlying investments ("portfolio companies," in the jargon). In fact, if a fund starts badly, it often requires more intensive management resources as each portfolio company takes more and more attention to turn it around. In those unhappy circumstances it could be against the fund investors' interests to pay lower fees, because without careful management the value can spiral down and the J curve can end up without a tail.

Of course, for the venture firm (the general partner) it is very nice to know that you can count on at least a fixed level of income for the first five years after raising one of these limited partnership funds. Once you have raised a fund of reasonable size you have an exceptionally steady business for the next five years. So if your Vulture turns to you in a board meeting and says "Well, we are always on budget; why aren't you?", you would be justified in pointing out to him that he has an unusually predictable business model.

A crunch normally comes after five or six years, at the end of the primary investment period, when the mechanism for calculating the fee may change. The 2.5% level may remain in place, but it will now often be calculated by reference to the original cost or the latest valuation of the investments remaining in the fund. In other words, any investments that have been successfully realized and any that have failed are subtracted. Unless the firm has delivered a strong enough performance to attract investors into its next fund and boost its fees by raising more money, this is a moment when it can feel a squeeze, when salaries and bonuses get reduced and staff are cut or leave.

Other types of fund pay fees in slightly different ways. Some venture capital funds are listed on a public stock exchange. These may be vehicles such as investment trusts, including venture capital trusts in the UK. They will normally levy their fees by reference to net asset value. So if a fund performs badly, valuations reduce and the manager's income will go down relative to that decline in value. You sometimes find that venture capital firms which manage listed funds are more resistant to marking down the value of their investments than those which have limited partnerships. Call me a cynic again, but this is for the simple reason that the former are hit where it hurts most by a valuation reduction – in their pockets – whereas the latter feel no immediate economic effect.

Other ways in which venture capital firms can earn income are by charging fees for fund raising; deal fees or corporate finance fees for making, organizing, and sometimes selling an investment; and directors' fees for joining portfolio company boards. In institutionally backed limited partnership funds these fees are generally offset in whole or in part against the management fee. The logic here is that the limited partnership investors do not want the Vulture to become rich from management fees, but from the profit share earned if he makes money for them. Nor do they want the managers' efforts to be diverted toward fee earning in order to make ends meet. So institutional investors may be more sympathetic toward a young firm which has not yet achieved critical mass from fund management fees alone; established firms are more likely to have to return all these miscellaneous fees to the fund.

Venture capitalists which manage other types of fund – once again including investment trusts and venture capital trusts, for example – are more likely to be able to keep all these miscellaneous fees. Fund-raising fees can be particularly important. Normally, for example, investors in a venture capital trust pay a 5% up-front fee for the privilege of investing in the fund. Some of this goes to pay brokers, accountants, lawyers, and other advisers, but for a firm which manages its affairs well, a good proportion can be kept out of the clutches of these professionals. This can be an important source of revenue.

So some of the behavior shown by venture capitalists can be explained by the type of funds they manage. A general partner may not bother to charge directors' fees or deal fees. When they are pitching for your business they may make great play of this, but they are not being generous. They are merely not too bothered because such fees have to be rebated to limited partners. A venture capital trust manager is likely to be rather keen on these fees; they may have a direct impact on his annual bonus. A long-established firm with plenty of fee income from funds under management may display an Olympian lack if interest in miscellaneous fees. A newer, smaller firm which has not yet ascended to these dizzy heights and tasted ambrosia may seem greedy for deal fees and directors' fees by comparison.

As a general rule, however, everything else pales into insignificance beside the fees on funds under management. Thus to prosper and grow, a venture capital firm, like any investment management business, has to increase its funds under management. This is a very challenging and highly competitive process. Only firms which deliver strong performance to their investors will be able to raise their next fund. This is why the medium-term focus of most venture capitalists is on making their funds perform well enough that they can raise the next one – or at least, on making it seem as if their funds are performing well enough to raise the next one.

There are some venture firms which have to give up all thought of raising another fund. When it becomes clear to the general partners that their fund will never make a positive return, and that their limited partners will not invest in their next vehicle (or "re-up," in the jargon), the current management fee may become their sole *raison d'être*. They become like an exploding supernova. If the younger members of the team, faced with no future, do not leave of their own volition, they may be blown out into the cold, as the senior partners seek to maximize the cash going into their own pockets while there is still time to milk the fees. These firms gradually disappear into their own black hole along with their investors' money.

Distributing proceeds

I described above how the limited partnership structure is designed to maximize internal rates of return by drawing down money from investors just before it is needed. Of course, the other side of this coin is that the realized coin needs to be distributed to limited partners as soon as possible. So when an investment is turned into cash as a result of a trade sale, or of the sale of shares listed on a stock exchange, the proceeds are normally paid back to the fund investors without much delay. Occasionally, realized profits are retained in the fund to cover management fees or follow-on investments, but this is a sign that the fund has become severely stretched and will do no favors to returns. Sometimes, when a company has achieved an IPO or stock exchange flotation, listed shares in the company are distributed to limited partners. (I talk in more detail about different types of exit in Chapter 12.)

These so-called distributions *in specie* are usually only made when an investment has been highly successful and become a large enough public company for there to be an active and liquid market for its shares. The limited partners will not mind receiving liquid stock which they can easily sell; they may well be large investors in listed equities themselves or have colleagues who are, and they may choose to hold the listed shares for more upside. But they are unlikely to be pleased about receiving a distribution of illiquid shares in a poxy little quoted company which may be impossible to sell all at once, or for some time; then the general partners will be seen as having ducked their responsibility and to have passed the problems associated with selling the shares back to their fund investors. In a couple of paragraphs' time I describe the profit share for which Vultures neurotically hope; this is calculated at the point at which the distribution is made to limited partners. So if a distribution *in specie* is made and then the share price of the company concerned collapses before the fund investors have been able to sell all their shares, they may feel somewhat aggrieved.

Other types of fund have different distribution policies. Some stock exchange-listed venture capital funds have a policy of paying out the majority of realized profits in lumpy dividends. Others might aim for a progressive dividend policy, with steadily rising distributions to shareholders, implying that they retain the bulk of each realization in the fund. These funds will reinvest some of the proceeds from realizations and have the aim of building up their net asset value (which, as noted above, increases their management fees), which should in turn push up the share price. However, the shares of most funds of this type trade at a discount to their net asset value, so if a shareholder wants to cash in by selling their shares, they are likely to have to do so at a price which is lower than the underlying assets are really worth.

Who is in charge?

Limited partnerships are carefully constructed so that there can be no comeback on limited partners beyond their investment in the fund. All the responsibility for managing the fund, for taking investment decisions, and any resultant liabilities, lies with the general partner. However, the limited partners will have considerable influence with the managers of the funds in which they invest, because those managers are likely to want them to invest in their next fund. Most GPs will avoid crossing their LPs, or taking unpopular decisions.

One area to which LPs are especially sensitive is a conflict of interest. These arise where a decision for one fund might clash with another area of the same venture capitalist's business. For example, if VC Fund I has invested in Xcorp, and Xcorp subsequently wants another round of funding, by which time the same venture capitalist has raised VC Fund II, whether VC Fund II should make an investment, and at what price, will give rise to a conflict of interest. Some of the investors in Fund I may not have invested in Fund II; some of them may have invested more or less as a proportion of the two funds; other investors may be new to Fund II. In each case, the LPs may have different relative economic interests. In these circumstances the view of an advisory committee is normally sought by the GP – and normally observed. The advisory committee is drawn from the largest and most prominent LPs in the relevant fund, sometimes supplemented by outsiders. They would also be consulted on other potentially controversial issues, such as valuations of investments for the annual accounts, and distributions *in specie*.

In most stock exchange-listed funds the roles are reversed. These funds are structured with a board which has similar legal obligations to any other group of directors and takes ultimate responsibility for the fund. Sometimes investment decision-making powers are delegated to the managers; sometimes they are formally taken by the board on the managers' advice.

Profit shares

Venture capitalists can make a pretty satisfactory living from their management fees. Unlike the entrepreneurs they back, they do not generally have to worry about closing that new sale next month to keep cash flow going to pay their salaries. The venture capital fund management business model has the attraction of being unusually stable and predictable. But how do Vultures hope to get rich? The answer is through their profit share on successful funds. In the jargon this is called the "carried interest," or "carry" for short. The normal way that carried interest works is that once a fund has returned its original cost to investors, typically plus a fixed annual return (a "hurdle rate"), the GPs receive 20% of the profits.

Supposedly this carried interest percentage and jargon orig-
inate from medieval Genoese, Pisan, Florentine, and Venetian
merchants, who carried cargoes belonging to others on their
ships in return for 20% of the ultimate profits. A few superstar
firms, modern Medicis, have been able to better even their
hard-nosed medieval antecedents, and increase their carried
interest percentage to 25% or 30%.

In a sense, even the more modest venture capital firms have
improved the model. For most firms, the percentage carry may
not have changed from the 500-year-old model. However, the
level of risk most certainly has. Those merchants often risked
life and limb in order to get a ride on the back of others' capital.
They owned the ships, and could suffer considerable loss if an
unexpected storm blew up, or if a skull and crossbones
appeared over the horizon. Today's venture capitalists only risk
a modest career setback if one of their funds goes underwater.
There is not yet much chance of being clapped in irons as a
galley slave by pirates marauding around Menlo Park.

The carry, the profit share that they leverage from their
investors' capital, is allocated between the members of the venture capital team on a pre-agreed basis. Note that usually the
carried interest depends on the performance of the whole fund,
not the performance of individual investments in that fund.
You only reach the end of this rainbow when all the failed
investments and all the management fees are netted off against
the successes. Thus in a venture capital team, the return of the
Vulture who backs more than his share of winners can be damaged by another member of the team who hoses away a fortune. The underperformer may not keep his place in the team.
Certainly, the star investor may push for – and win – a larger
share of the carry in the next fund.

In modern times, though, this consideration is often an academic one. I would wager a good portion of the carried interest
that I have earned in the past that a majority of current venture
capital practitioners, certainly those who were first cut into the

carry after the millennium, have never found that pot of gold. Most have never enjoyed the sweet pleasure of cashing a carried interest check.

This is because making money from venture capital investment is a truly challenging process. Remember here the distinction I made between venture capital and private equity. Remember too that the first decade of the current century has been especially difficult for early-stage and technology investing. No sooner had the fall-out from the bursting of the internet bubble in 2000/01 largely decayed than another nuclear explosion occurred in the shape of the 2008 global economic crisis.

Venture capital funds are usually measured according to vintage. Those hostile to the industry might say that this is just to give successful general partners the excuse to hold forth about their extensive collections of Premiers Crus Clarets and the vast, temperature-controlled cellars they have had to construct beneath their ranches or country houses to accommodate them. I have suffered quite a few conversations along those lines, but actually measuring funds by vintage year is fair enough. Like most asset classes, the performance of venture capital funds is inextricably linked to the era in which they are invested. So performance in the run-up to the bubble of 1999 and 2000 tended to be strong; funds raised in 1995–97 were also frequently fine performers. Funds invested at the top of the cycle, even by famous investors, have not necessarily reached the end of their lives, but when they have, most partners – both limited and general – will want to forget about them. Remember that vintages are named by the year in which they are raised and start investing; the investment process will mostly take between two and three years to complete, perhaps up to five. A 1995 vintage fund, therefore, would be invested largely in 1995–97.

Unfortunately, it seems to be one of the immutable laws of venture capital that the largest volume of money is raised and invested at precisely the wrong place in the cycle. So the volume of capital available rose sharply around 1987, just in time to be damaged by the economic difficulties at the start of the 1990s. In the first half of the 1990s, because of weak performance, less money was raised, and then stellar performance from the 1995 and 1996 vintages attracted absurd volumes of capital in 1999 and 2000, which was invested wildly at the top of the market. So perhaps it really is rather like wine: the best vintages tend to be small and very few really special vineyards produce good wine every year.

The British Private Equity and Venture Capital Association, or BVCA for short, publishes an annual review of the performance of its members' funds based on work done by Fund of Funds manager Capital Dynamics and accountants PricewaterhouseCoopers. The performance of early-stage funds of different vintage bands is shown in the table below in terms of the performance measurement normally used in the industry, the internal rate of return, or compound annual return to investors.

Vintage	Median IRR p.a.	25th percentile IRR p.a.
1997	7.1%	18.6%
1998	N/A	N/A
1999	−7.6%	3.6%
2000	−8.1%	0.1%
2001	−8.3%	−3.3%
2002	−11.6%	2.0%
2003	−0.7%	2.5%
2004	N/A	N/A
2005	−11.9%	0.0%

Source: BVCA Private Equity and Venture Capital Performance Measurement Survey 2009.

With a negative median return for every vintage year except 1997, these statistics show that most funds in the sample actually lost money. The top 25% (the 25th percentile shows the bottom of this range) from the 1997 vintage performed pretty well. Clearly, the performance of the best funds would have outperformed even this number. However, from the 1998 vintage onward, the lowest of the best 25% has done little more than give investors their money back. Of course, once again the best funds from these vintages will have done better. I should also point out that many of the funds from later vintages will not yet have reached the end of their lives. Some of this performance data is therefore based on valuations, not realizations, and may get better as these funds finally mature.

I hear North American readers thinking: "Ah, but in the US venture capital makes more money." It hurts me as a European to have to admit the truth of that statement, but the difference is not as great as some might think. Or at least, the overall performance pattern of the industry in the US is similar. The statistics below are compiled by investment adviser Cambridge Associates

Vintage	Median IRR p.a.	25th percentile IRR p.a.
1995	42.9%	81.4%
1996	33.2%	92.1%
1997	8.6%	56.1%
1998	−1.2%	18.5%
1999	−5.4%	2.5%
2000	−3.5%	2.9%
2001	−0.4%	6.0%
2002	−1.7%	4.8%
2003	1.8%	4.2%
2004	−1.6%	2.5%
2005	−2.2%	4.2%

Source: Cambridge Associates LLC, U.S. Venture Capital Index and Selected Benchmark Statistics, Non-Marketable Alternative Assets, December 31, 2009.

and published by the National Venture Capital Association or NVCA for short. They may be compiled in a slightly different way to the BVCA statistics but are broadly comparable.

Essentially these show that in the US, median returns have usually been a bit worse and the 25th percentile a bit better than the 25th percentile returns in the UK, and have been negative every year since 1997 except for 2003.

As previously noted, these statistics demonstrate a very wide range between the firms that perform well and those that do not. Firms that have a poor track record are understandably coy about revealing how much money they have lost. But one of the peculiarities of the industry is that the superstar firms like Kleiner Perkins and Sequoia Capital are even more coy about admitting how good their performance really is. A storm erupted in the industry in 2003 when freedom of information legislation obliged some limited partners with a public-sector connection to publish the performance of the funds in which they had invested. Some of these unfortunate LPs were excluded from future funds, but not before they were forced to reveal data which makes one's mouth water. For example, the next table, showing the multiples achieved by Kleiner Perkins on its funds, was published by the University of California in 2005.

Fund	Vintage year	Multiple on cost	Estimated IRR
KP II	1980	4.30x	51%
KP III	1982	1.74x	10%
KP IV	1986	1.83x	11%
KP V	1989	4.01x	36%
KP VI	1992	3.33x	39%
KP VII	1994	32.51x	122%
KP VIII	1996	17.00x	287%
KP IX	1999	0.40x	−23%
KP X	2000	0.59x	−18%

The last two funds in the table were only partway through their life in 2005, and, if only because of its investment in Google, the 1999 vintage fund must by now have defied the cycle. But the most striking numbers in this table are the performances of Funds VII and VIII. You could perhaps criticize Kleiner Perkins's brand management skills in allowing itself to sound like a well-known marque of peanuts, but you cannot criticize this spectacular performance. For most Vultures, 17× cost on one investment is a major achievement, and 32.5× is a dream (my personal best is 50×). To achieve that result on a fund overall is just extraordinary.

Benchmark Capital, one of the younger members of the "top tier," is the firm which is reputed to have delivered the best performance on a fund. Its first fund, of the 1995 vintage, supposedly achieved a $2.5 billion return, or a modest 500 times cost, on its $5 million investment in eBay. The 2006 Private Equity Performance Monitor reports a multiple for the fund of 42× – or almost $4.25 billion on its $101 million cost. So while eBay accounts for a bit more than half of that, there must have been a few other good investments too.

Thus it is possible for venture capitalists to make a great deal of money from the carried interest. If the firm starts with a $100 million fund and trebles it after deducting fees – a strong but not staggering performance – there will be 20% of $200 million – $40 million – to share out between the general partners. A fund of $100 million might sustain a firm of four partners, so that is $10 million each, or $1 million for each year of a 10-year fund. These may not be modern investment banking-type bonuses, but they are more than enough to be getting along with.

The really successful venture capital investors, the ones who deliver extraordinary results, like Kleiner Perkins, Benchmark, and Sequoia, make extraordinary sums of money – and rightly so, for they are genuinely contributing to the wealth-creation process. Kleiner Perkins's Funds VII and VIII were $225 million and $315 million in size respectively, and their carried interest percentage was 30%. So the multiples of 17 and 32 times, as attributed by the University of California data, could have generated a carried interest pool on these two funds of $1.1 billion and $2.9 billion respectively. The LPs must have thought that their KP GP had earned every cent of it.

Raising the next fund

Sequoia, Kleiner Perkins, Benchmark, and the handful of other superstar firms in their peer group – the famous "top tier" – have no difficulty raising their next fund. In fact, quite the reverse: it is almost impossible for new investors to gain access to them. As the general partners accumulate wealth, they are likely to want to invest more of their own money in their funds, squeezing down outside investors. They made their bubble-era funds too big, and in some cases they reduced their LPs' commitments to those funds. They are too smart to make the same mistake again. Increasing the size of a fund too far damages performance because it increases the supply of capital beyond the supply of good deals, and forces GPs to expand their investment team excessively and dilute their talent. So in these top-tier funds, a minor transgression by an investor, one small complaint, one due diligence question too many, or one small delay in responding to a drawdown request may lead to his being unceremoniously ejected from the investor group. However, there are precious few superstar firms that can behave like this. Very few hold the whip hand over their investors. Most firms handle their actual and potential fund investors with kid-gloved respect.

So just how competitive is it for a venture capital firm to raise its next fund? It always used to be said that with a net compound annual return of above 20% the next fund should not be a problem, and that with a return in the high teens you would probably be all right. The NVCA and BVCA data above suggest that not too many firms can demonstrate that sort of performance. Even being in the top quartile – among the best 25% of their peer group – may not be good enough. Limited partners often joke that they have never met a venture capital investor who claims to be anything other than top quartile and question whether such creatures exist, but by definition three-quarters of investors are not top quartile, and at least three-quarters will therefore struggle to raise their next fund. As well as comparing one GP with another, potential LPs look at absolute returns and will expect a premium return over comparable asset classes because of the higher risk, higher volatility, and lower liquidity inherent in a venture capital fund.

After 2007–08, with returns on almost every asset class devastated, investors should perhaps be a little more forgiving – but they themselves have less money to invest. They have probably become more risk averse. The fact therefore remains that for most venture capital firms, delivering a strong enough performance to raise the next fund is very challenging. The successful investments in a fund have to overcome the drag of the failures, and of the management fees. Those fees may be important for putting regular food on the Vulture's table, but over a fund's 10-year life they will themselves gobble up nearly 25% of the capital.

Portfolio construction

All of this has major implications for how venture capital investors view your business. Different venture firms have different approaches to risk and reward and to how they construct a portfolio to deliver an acceptable return to their investors. Some, probably including the best firms of all, may rely on a small number of very big winners, investments which return not just tens of times cost, but hundreds of times cost. In the past they have made investments that have achieved very high multiples; they have confidence that they can do so again. But they also know that such things cannot realistically be modeled. Their approach is likely to be more instinctive, more focused on sniffing out and executing large opportunities than on measuring and defining them at the beginning.

For those firms that do attempt to model their portfolio in a systematic way, a not uncommon theoretical approach is to divide it into three categories: the losers, the living dead, and the winners. Say each category forms 25% of the fund, with the remaining 25% reserved to pay management fees. Say investments are made evenly over four years, and realized evenly five years after investment. Say losers return nothing, and the living dead return cost.

The table overleaf assumes a $100 million fund on this basis and shows the cash flow to and from the fund investors. Negative numbers are cash that they pay out; positive numbers show money paid back to them from the fund. The table shows that in order for fund investors to achieve a 20% compound annual return net of fees and carried interest, the average multiple on cost of the winners must be nine times cost. Note, by the way, that, taking into consideration the management fee and the carry, the general partner ends up with almost half of the original amount committed to the fund – $49 million out of $100 million – for a performance that is good but not stellar.

Many venture capital investors have never achieved a 9× return on any single investment, let alone achieved that average across their winners. Over five years, that multiple of nine times the cost of an investment equates to an internal rate of return on that investment of 55%.

This model is, of course, simplistic. Different firms have their own, more sophisticated approaches, but broadly the same principle applies. An investor using a similar model will need to back businesses which have the potential to deliver nine or ten times the cost of the investment in five years, or an IRR of 55–60%. While that is quite a tall order, that is the sort of yardstick against which the potential of your business will be measured.

ANGELS, DRAGONS AND VULTURES

Cash flow ($m)	Y1	Y2	Y3	Y4	Y5	Y6	Y7	Y8	Y9	Total
Fees	−2.50	−2.50	−2.50	−2.50	−2.50	−2.50	−2.50	−2.50	−2.50	−22.50
Investment in losers	−6.25	−6.25	−6.25	−6.25						−25.00
Return on losers						0.00	0.00	0.00	0.00	0.00
Investment in living dead	−6.25	−6.25	−6.25	−6.25						−25.00
Return on living dead						6.25	6.25	6.25	6.25	25.00
Investment in winners	−6.25	−6.25	−6.25	−6.25						−25.00
Return on winners						56.25	56.25	56.25	56.25	225.00
Carried interest							−4	−11.25	−11.25	−26.50
Cash flow to LPs	−21.25	−21.25	−21.25	−21.25	−2.50	60.00	56.00	48.75	48.75	126.00
IRR to LPs										20.22%
Multiple on winners										9.00x
Multiple on fund										2.63x
Total multiple to LPs										2.50x
Cash return to GP										49.00

Your own Mephistopheles

Anxious Faustian entrepreneurs need to be aware of all these generic pressures on their investors. They also need to be aware of the individual pressures on their personal Mephistopheles, because the generic pressures on the GP will be compounded by the pressures placed by the GP firm on the individual who did their deal.

In particular, the younger members of the team in a venture firm may have never tasted success. They may have never made an investment which has moved through to a trade sale exit, let alone to an initial public offering (IPO) or stock market flotation. They are likely to be under considerable pressure to achieve these successes. Pressure may be manifested in very tangible ways. Many venture firms will have a good reserve of profits from their management fees at the end of the year after paying their fixed overheads. While the senior partners, the founders of the firm, will probably snaffle a large proportion of any excess, some at least will go into a bonus pool for the rest of the team. One of the factors in determining how this is allocated may be the performance of the investments for which each individual is responsible. Certainly performance will affect each individual's position in the firm. In the nearer term this may be limited to status, but over time it will also have an impact on promotion, on admission to the partnership or to the board, and on the allocation of profit share or carried interest. Normally carried interest in a fund is allocated across the investment team according to position and seniority. Occasionally it is linked to the specific deals done by each individual. But usually if someone has done well and shown himself to be a proven money-maker, he will achieve his ambition of being cut into the carry, or his share of the carry in the next fund will go up.

So if things are going badly in your company and your personal Vulture seems devilishly bad-tempered, remember that he may feel in a very personal way that you are costing him money, wrecking his ability to educate his children, or blighting his career.

The customer and the product

I hope it is clear by now who is the Vulture's customer. Some Vultures talk about the companies in which they invest as their customer, but this is at best careless and at worst disingenuous. The companies in which Vultures invest are the products they offer to their real customers, their fund investors. And of course, the "customer is king." (I did once work for a business whose main customer really was called King, which caused much hilarity all round and led to posters bearing that slogan being pinned up all around the workplace.)

So do not make the mistake of thinking that *you* are the customer, the most important person in the Vulture's network of relationships. You are the Vulture's product. And remember that you, as an individual, are not even the whole product, but only part of it. The Vulture's whole product range is made up of all the companies in which he has invested or will invest, and each of those products has a number of components: the management team, the technology, the market opportunity, its own product or service, and so on.

Of course the Vulture's product is important to him, just as your product is important to you. But just as you can and will – or at least should – adapt your product to meet your customers' needs, so the Vulture will try to adapt his product, pressing to change the focus of a portfolio company, or altering the management team, making whatever changes are necessary to make it more attractive to their customer – in this case more successful and more profitable for their investor.

You may have a number of SKUs (stock-keeping units) in your product range. Some may be much more important than others, either because they are outselling the rest, or because they generate a better margin, or perhaps because you have invested so much in developing them that you cannot afford to let them fail. On the other hand, you may have some products which generate little revenue, no profit, and, thank heavens, have not cost you very much. You probably don't pay much attention to those ones and they may get discontinued.

A Vulture's investment portfolio is little different to your product range. He hopes to have some companies which are doing well. These will represent a high proportion of the value in the portfolio. Some of these may have been small investments which have done exceptionally well; these are clearly the highest-margin products. And he may have some investments whose cost is so high that he simply cannot afford to let them fail. All of these will take most of his attention, and he will spend less time on the products – companies – in which he has not invested very much, and whose prospects are not very interesting.

THE ANGELS (AND DRAGONS)

The Vultures invest other people's money. The Angels invest their own. So it is no surprise that their attitudes are a little different.

You would have to be a very holy Angel indeed not to mind losing money. Nevertheless, it can be easier to lose your own money than somebody else's. No sensible Angel will invest more than he can afford to lose. He may have taken that risk earlier in his career in the business activity that made him enough money to act as an Angel now, but he will not invest more than he can afford to lose in somebody else's business. Most of his wealth now will probably be allocated to asset classes that are a great deal safer than venture capital.

Nor does an Angel have to worry about management fees. He does not lose sleep about achieving an IRR good enough to enable him to raise the next fund, or about the impact of a bad investment on his career prospects. That is all behind him. The average Angel is probably more worried about his wife complaining about the amount of time he is spending on a particular investment, or his friends muttering in the clubhouse, "Mike's latest deal is turning sour. He must be losing his touch."

That is not to say that Angels behave in an uncommercial way. Their business antennae are likely to be far more sensitive than a young Vulture's. (You would be correct to point out that young Vultures do not have antennae at all, but nor, as far as I know, do Angels, so my metaphor has completely broken down.) Your Angel will want to cut a good deal. He may want to charge you a director's fee, but not so much because he needs the money as from the fairly reasonable point of view that it is poor discipline to do something for nothing, and that if he does not charge you a fee his contribution may not be properly valued.

If an Angel's investment does go wrong, the tax system can often apply salve to his wounds. If he makes a capital loss he may well have gains elsewhere against which it can be offset. In some tax regimes, such as the UK, even if he has no balancing capital gains, he may be able to offset a loss against income tax at his highest marginal rate. If he has invested with the benefit of the Enterprise Incentive Scheme, or EIS, the British tax man's generosity currently means that he cannot lose more than 30% of his total investment. You look surprised? That is because under the EIS you get 20% income tax relief and 18% capital gains tax roll-over relief up front, so your investment costs only 62% of face value. If you lose everything, you can offset the 80% on which you did not get income tax relief against your highest rate of 40%, effectively getting back another 32% (80% × 40%). So provided that you can roll over your capital gains tax liability again, only 30% of the original investment cost remains unsheltered. The Inland Revenue has paid for the other 70%. In some instances, if you have an earlier capital gain taxable at the old rate of 40%, the maximum loss declines to 8% of the total, with the tax authorities funding the remaining 92% (20% + (80% × 40%) + 40%). By the time you read this book the tax rates may have changed so I apologize if my figures are out of date; however, the principle that a portion of the cost of an investment in a private company can be attractively sheltered is unlikely to have changed.

Anyway, part of an Angel's motivation will most probably be for the sport. That is not to say for a moment that Angels are likely to be a soft touch; in fact, frequently quite the reverse. Often because they have worked hard for their money and therefore know its value, because they have built companies themselves, and because generally they only invest in businesses they understand, they may be more aggressive than a Vulture about getting stuck into yours (and into you) if they think you're doing a poor job. If you are doing a poor job that may not be such a bad thing.

However, they are unlikely to give you a hard time over petty matters. Many Angels (dare I say the best Angels?) have been entrepreneurs. If so, they have often had Vultures of their own to deal with. So they can be better at not loading you with the irritations sometimes caused by institutional investors who have not been on the entrepreneur's side of the fence. They may tend to take a simpler and longer-term view of capital structures and equity incentives. They may avoid getting unnecessarily bogged down in some of the awkward remuneration issues I discuss in Chapter 7. Like the more experienced chess player, they may be better at realizing that snatching that exposed pawn now and gaining a short-term advantage from going one piece up is in fact a mistake because of what is likely to happen five moves later.

You will see that implicit in this is the definition of the Angel as an experienced businessperson, actively involved in the businesses he backs. In this sense, the Angel is a Dragon. There are Angel investment groups which operate by sourcing funding from multiple private investors, and Angel funds with limited partnership structures which source their capital from private individuals instead of institutions. There is nothing wrong with these, but it is important to understand that they may be different in some respects to having a direct investment from an Angel and a simple one-on-one relationship. In some cases Angel funds make a point of tapping into the individual expertise of their investors and thus deliver Angelic benefits by using a member of their network to manage individual investments. Nevertheless, as soon as a third party becomes involved, managing somebody else's money, the dynamics grow more complicated, and some of the features attributed to Vultures earlier in this chapter may emerge.

Otherwise, as you would expect, the disadvantages of working with an Angel – or a Dragon – rather than a Vulture are those of working with an individual rather than a firm. Everything depends on a single relationship; if it sours, or something goes wrong, there is nobody else to turn to. If you find that you can no longer stomach your personal Vulture, at least you can call up his boss. Ringing God to complain about your Angel is not possible.

And because an Angel can afford to lose the money he has invested, because he is investing in part for sport, because he no longer has career pressures to worry about, he may be able to walk away from an investment and draw a line under it more easily than a Vulture could. His personal circumstances may also change, or he may get bored and decide to extricate himself because he is no longer enjoying it.

Finally, most Angels will not be able or willing to invest as much as a Venture Capital fund. The Dragons in their den normally talk in terms of tens of thousands, sometimes hundreds of thousands, but almost never millions. If you are going to need millions to fund your business, you are unlikely to be able to get it all from an Angel. At some point you will have to go to the Vultures. However, the amount they invest, together with the expertise and support they provide, often make Angels the most appropriate source for the first injection of outside capital in your business.

Certainly, many of the best investments I made in my career as a Vulture were when I invested in the round after an Angel investment. I enjoyed working with these experienced businesspeople and learned a great deal from them. They helped me to contain some of my youthful Vulturish tendencies and to rub some of the rough edges off my beak. If I were starting out now to set up a business for the first time, I would aim to get a wise Angel investor to spread his wings around me before I approached any Vultures.

CHAPTER THREE

Raising Money Successfully

*So you plan to take the plunge:
how do you avoid a belly flop?*

I cannot dive. Every so often on holiday I cause my family great hilarity by trying to do so. However hard I try, whatever I do, I simply cannot get my legs properly straight. The angle of attack remains hopelessly oblique. So I may have chosen the wrong metaphor for this chapter. But at least I always check there is water in the pool before I jump.

THE ODDS

In the firm where I used to work, about 1,000 investment propositions crossed our threshold every year. That is 20 each week, 4 every working day. Most of those ended up on the desks of five people. Given that two-thirds of the team's time was taken up with managing existing investments, and perhaps one sixth with marketing, investor relations, and business development, scarcely one sixth of our time – the equivalent of one full-time individual – was available to handle this torrent of investment propositions and to make new investments. This type of ratio is not unusual for the industry.

We rejected approximately half of the incoming plans immediately, on the grounds that some simple criteria excluded them: size, location, stage, or sector. Or they might simply be completely batty.

The other 500 were entered in a database – called in the inevitable industry jargon the "deal log" – and given more of a read. About another half were rejected after that. Preliminary meetings would be held with the rest. In a normal year we might make ten new investments, two for each active member of the investment team. If we did many more we would feel that we had been exceptionally busy. So for the entrepreneurs coming to us for money, the success rate fell to somewhere around 1%.

Of course, quite a few of these businesses went on to find funding elsewhere, from firms with different investment criteria and different preferences. The statistics quoted by selective schools and colleges – 500 applicants for only 10 places, or whatever – always make it sound more difficult to get in than it really is, because of course there are other schools down the road for which the same applicants are trying. And naturally, just like the brightest pupils, the best entrepreneurs might have several offers and decide to turn us down in favor of going elsewhere. Nevertheless, it is a highly competitive process.

IMPROVING THE ODDS

We had a policy of responding to every proposal we received. In most cases this involved sending out a standard rejection letter or email. Quite a lot of firms do not respond at all to a cold call, so the best way of improving your chances of raising money is to make sure that you have a way in.

Our attention (and I do not imagine that other firms are very different) was best grabbed by the following, in order of effectiveness:

1 An entrepreneur we had successfully backed before (one of our heroes) coming back a second time as part of a team.
2 One of our heroes introducing a team and giving them a strong recommendation.
3 A team headed by a stranger with a proven track record of making money (somebody else's hero).

4 A professional – a lawyer, accountant, or broker – with whom we had previously worked making an introduction.
5 A proposal which hit a sweet spot in a sector that we happened to be targeting at that moment.
6 A really compelling and well-argued business plan.

Some of this is about courtesy and human nature, of course, about returning favors and scratching backs. But it is also about improving the ratio between risk and reward. The involvement of a known quantity is an obvious way for an investor to reduce uncertainty and thus lower the perceived level of risk while increasing the perceived potential reward.

It follows, therefore, that if you are doing this for the first time, bring into your team someone who has done it before, if you possibly can. If you cannot bring them formally into your team, co-opt them as a mentor and adviser.

This is part of the reason for the preference I expressed at the end of the previous chapter for getting an Angel involved – or even a Dragon – before you attempt to attract a Vulture. This individual might be an ideal candidate to act as your chairman. Bringing in a chairman, who to be worth his salt will himself be quite a big beast, may go against your grain and feel as if you are ceding an unnecessary element of control. But don't feel like that.

The benefits brought by a good chairman will be a *leitmotif* of subsequent chapters. Certainly one of the common characteristics of most of the successful investments in which I have been involved has been a good independent chairman – and that is good for the investor obviously, but also for the entrepreneur.

However, before you can attract a chairman, an Angel, or a Vulture, you have to have a business plan.

YOUR BUSINESS PLAN – FACT OR FICTION?

Some venture capital firms have a section on their website saying what they expect to see in a business plan. Some, perhaps anxious at least to appear to offer a friendly face and a helping hand, even provide a template for entrepreneurs to fill in. I have always taken a different view: to me, if an entrepreneur does not understand his own business well enough to know what to put into his plan, then he does not deserve to raise money. (For a similar reason, by the way, I have always disliked business plans prepared by professionals. I do not want to know how the minds of those excellent accountants at KPMG or PWC work; I know *they* can write a business plan. I want to know if entrepreneurs I am considering backing can write a business plan, and from that plan I want to gain an insight into the way they think.)

So you will not find in this book a list of things you should put in your business plan. I repeat, if you do not know what is important about your business, you do not deserve to raise money and you may as well stop reading now.

But I am going to give you a few tips, because the business plan you need for fundraising is unfortunately a bit different to the plan you need to run your business.

If your fundraising business plan were a person, they would probably be shut up in a secure institution. At the very least they would be spending a large slice of their time on the shrink's couch.

This is because fundraising business plans have seriously split personalities. On the one hand, they have to be what they say they are: a genuine plan for the business; one, incidentally, whose fairness and reasonableness you will have to warrant in your Stock Purchase or Shareholders' Agreement, and against which you will be measured later if you succeed in raising money. On the other hand, they are marketing documents, designed to entice the Angel, Dragon, or Vulture to part with his money on terms that are attractive to you.

The Vultures, and perhaps even some Angels or Dragons, compound this problem, because the first thing they do to your business plan is to divide all your projected revenue numbers by two. This knee-jerk reaction is perhaps not totally unreasonable, because it is based on their actual experience that all the businesses they have backed in the past took twice as long and consumed twice as much money to get half as far as the original business plan suggested. It is hard to break this vicious circle. You will not be able to persuade them that you are the first that will be different.

Thus you have to walk a difficult tightrope. The plan has to be realistic and credible, but also capable of being significantly scaled back and still showing attractive investment returns.

THE FACT

During the period when you are talking to investors, you must be able to overachieve on your plan. I am afraid to say that often investors will spin out their process deliberately so that they can test whether you will meet your plan, and to verify whether you will do what you say you are going to do. If you fall short, your credibility, and by extension the credibility of the rest of the plan, will be undermined. The thinking goes as follows: if they cannot set a budget and achieve it in the near term of which they should have reasonable visibility, how on earth are they going to get close to what they say they will do in a year's time? So if you fall short of your budget during the three- or six-month capital-raising period, you run the risk of blowing the deal completely, or at least of causing its terms to deteriorate seriously. During this period of courtship it is vital that you do better than you say you will; then you will keep the investor sweet and be able to lead him up the aisle.

In the financial period immediately after investment, it is also important to your new relationship with your investor that you continue to achieve expectations. You do not want your honeymoon to be curtailed or to end on a sour note. You do not want your new partner to begin shooting sideways looks at you. You do not want unspoken recriminations hanging in the air. That can lead to an early divorce, and you may not be the one who keeps the house.

Therefore, be genuinely conservative about the early part of your plan.

THE FICTION

Unfortunately, if you apply the same principle to its later stages, you may be underselling yourself, which could just as easily destroy your chances of raising investment. Your financial plan must be bold enough to look exciting even after it's been scaled back by your cynical Vulture.

How exciting is exciting enough? In the previous chapter I explained that the main pressure on most Vultures is to deliver returns good enough to make it possible to raise their next fund, and that a net compound annual return of 20% should do the job. I also explained that to deliver this return across the board, the successful investments have to be theoretically able to multiply their cost close to tenfold. That is after your financial projections have been downgraded or detuned to make them more "realistic."

With some investors, the ones who construct their portfolios in a more risk-averse way, so that they avoid so many losses and aim to generate their returns mostly from steadier multiples of five and six times, you may get away with a lower theoretical return. To do so you will have to persuade them that your plan is relatively low risk, which is only possible if you already have a steady business.

But however they plan their portfolio, few genuine venture investors will make an investment on a planned internal rate of return of less than 40%. After four years, that is 3.8 times cost; after five, 5.4 times. Perhaps one or two will look at a theoretical return of 30% (3.7 times cost after five years), but only if they really consider the risks to be low.

You need to look at your business plan through Vultures' eyes and make sure that, even downgraded, it can deliver this sort of return off the entry valuation that you are seeking.

And if that seems the wrong way around, you can take consolation from the fact that even the most inexperienced Vulture will concede that a plan running out four or five years can only be an illustrative indication of what might happen.

This is my business plan adage:

Fiction can lead to friction.
But fact does not always get backed.

SANITY CHECKS

For all that, the plan must be believable. Carry out some simple sanity checks. Look at the publicly available information on companies in the same sector as you and comparable in size to what you hope to become. If your plan shows a much higher level of steady-state profitability than is the norm, there is probably something wrong with it. Pre-tax profit of over 35% of revenue is not the norm for the software industry, for example; it is what Microsoft and one or two other outliers achieve.

Check how the percentage of revenue or gross margin you plan to spend on the main functional areas – sales, marketing, research and development, and finance and administration – compares with the sector norm. If you are out of line, and there is no justifiable reason for it, you have got something wrong. Think again and adjust your numbers. Make sure that your revenue and fully loaded costs per employee are credible, and that the trends from year to year are what you would expect.

Over and over again I've met entrepreneurs whose plans showed levels of profitability attained only by a fraction of market-leading companies, and who were unaware of their error. Be ready with examples to justify all the key assumptions you are making. If your investment case depends on a multiple at exit of 20 times profit, you will be laughed out of court unless you can point to other companies which have achieved the same. Likewise, if you project year-on-year sales growth of 50%, you should be ready with examples of peers and competitors which have done as well.

In my experience, this poor correlation between the business plan and the real world is the most common weakness of investment propositions. The next most frequent flaw is a lack of knowledge and information about competitors and markets. Business plans which claim to have no competitors deserve to go straight into the shredder, both because of the likely naïvety they display and because even if it is a correct assumption, you cannot build a business unless you create some competition. There may have been no spreadsheet before Visicalc; but Visicalc competed with the slide rule, the calculator, and customized computer programs. There always has to be a competitor, otherwise you are claiming to be able to get people to do something they have never done before, and after millennia of evolution that is a tall order indeed. Getting people to do the same thing in a different way is hard enough.

This broad view of the competitive landscape can also help with the tricky issue of market size. Even the very best industry analysts have clouds in their crystal balls, the main fault of which always seems to be to predict that a new way of doing things will gain wide adoption far sooner than it really can in practice. How you define your market is important. To many investors, especially in technology markets, you will be of more interest if your objective is to become one of the market leaders: if not the "gorilla" with a 30–40% share, at least one of the "monkeys" at 15–20%. The rapid pace of technology innovation typically means that market share is concentrated in the hands of a small number of successful companies. Market leadership helps to justify a premium price at exit. Nevertheless, for market leadership to be a credible objective, you will need a tight definition of the market on which you plan to focus – while not, of course, being such a tight definition that the market size will be too small to deliver the returns your incoming investor needs.

LESSONS OF HISTORY

Although in theory investors will choose to back you primarily on the basis of what your business might be worth in the future, history also plays its part in determining whether they will invest and on what terms. Different Vultures (and Angels or Dragons) will have their own rules of thumb – their own sanity checks – that they will apply to your historical performance. If you generated $1 million or $2 million of revenue last year, they will use that as a reference point for their valuation.

My valuation rule of thumb in the software sector was a maximum of three times historical revenue. When I deserted that in the bubble years, I generally came to regret it.

If you are a pre-revenue start-up, raising your first investment round, it may not be possible to derive a valuation from your past performance, but the investors you talk to will have a price range at which they are prepared to do a Series A investment, and outside which they are unlikely to stray.

HOW MUCH TO RAISE

You might think that the amount of capital you should aim to raise follows simply from your business plan. The plan shows that you have a cash shortfall of $2,678,324 in month 19, and that thereafter cash flow turns positive so that the negative balance reduces and then substantial amounts build up in the balance sheet. So you set out to raise $2,678,324 plus a margin for error, say $3 million.

Well... not necessarily. Depending on the nature of your business and the stage it has reached, it may be right to raise the whole amount in one go. On the other hand, if you are a start-up, or your technology is little more than a bright idea, it may cost you too much of your equity to raise the full amount up front. Or you may be unable to find an investor willing to risk the whole amount at such an early stage. So perhaps you consider raising $500,000 at first, to take you past some important milestones such as the production of a prototype, or the opening of your first retail outlet. It will be easier to find an investor to risk that amount and the percentage equity you sell may be reduced. When you are further down the track, and certain key assumptions are proven, you can then raise the balance with more certainty and on better terms.

Particularly in investment-hungry industries such as biotech or semiconductors, where $20 million, or $50 million, or even $100 million is needed to take a business all the way through to exit, it is almost unheard of to raise the full amount of money at the outset. The norm is a number of investment rounds: the seed round, then the Series A, Series B, Series C, and sometimes ever deeper into the alphabet. Your original investor is likely to have to contribute something to each round, with new investors often joining at each stage, and then following on subsequently. (The intricacies of later funding rounds are discussed in Chapter 11.)

Judging the right amount to raise at each point is not easy. If you raise too little you may find yourself devoting far too much of your precious time to fund raising, and failing to pass the milestones which give you an uplift in value. If you raise too much you can suffer excessive dilution, and also make the equation less attractive for investors, thus reducing the likelihood of securing investment. Overall, remember that equity is the most expensive form of funding you can raise. Save every dollar you can by cutting corners. Beg and borrow equipment (perhaps draw the line at stealing). Squeeze into the smallest amount of cheap office space that you can. Apart from creating a healthy business culture, by being as frugal as possible you are likely to enhance your own returns and your investors'.

TO SYNDICATE OR NOT TO SYNDICATE?

Perhaps you thought that you would simply raise the amount you settled on from one investor. Again, the answer to that is maybe... or maybe not. In the era before the technology bubble burst, first rounds with single investors were relatively common. There was confidence in the air and if a business progressed, it should be possible to raise more money at a higher price from new investors. So the first-round investor could go in at a lower valuation, take a higher proportion of the equity for his money, and end up making better returns than the second-round investor. After all, the first-round investor takes a higher risk, over a longer period, therefore needs a higher return to make sense of his model.

However, after the technology bubble burst in 2000, the venture world became a more cautious place and the supply of capital got far tighter. Second-round investors were able to come in at prices lower than the first-round investors. Third-round investors were able to invest on more attractive terms than second-round investors, and so on. So the people taking the least risk often ended up making the best returns. (I return to the collateral damage caused by these "down rounds" in Chapter 11.)

This caused early-stage investors to reassess their strategy, and in the less exuberant noughties it became more normal for investments to be syndicated at the seed or Series A stage, even when relatively small amounts of money were involved. The early-stage investors became focused more on the risk than the return, and prefer to protect against the downside by sharing an exciting opportunity. Then, if progress is slow, or if the investment climate becomes colder, and new investors are not interested on acceptable terms, the original syndicate has deep enough pockets to fund the company further.

For the entrepreneur, that makes the money-raising challenge potentially greater because instead of exciting just one Angel, Dragon, or Vulture, you have to thrill two, or three, or four. Sometimes one can be edged into the position of lead investor and can help with the process of assembling the syndicate, but the initial complexities undoubtedly increase.

Sometimes having a broadly based investor group can help later on, however. If one of the investor group falls by the wayside, loses faith in you, or runs out of money, the others *might* continue their support. Your eggs are not all in one basket. Or sometimes (with apologies for mixing my grocery store metaphors) one rotten apple in the barrel turns the others bad, and the investor with the weakest nerves infects the rest.

LOOK BEFORE YOU LEAP

You have decided on your financing strategy. Your plan is perfected. You are sure you can overachieve against budget in the early months. You are confident that you will meet the first year's target. There is enough padding in the later years to withstand brutal sensitivities and still make a venture return possible without selling an unacceptable proportion of your equity.

You have had the introductions you needed. You know how to get from Buckingham Gate to St. James's Street and you know which way the numbers run up Sand Hill Road (from East to West, as it happens). You have your meetings set up. You are ready.

Look before you leap always seems to me to be good advice. But that means really look. It always used to surprise me how many of the entrepreneurs who came to me for money had scarcely even glanced over the edge of the cliff. Very few had really stared all the way to the bottom. Maybe they didn't dare, but they gave the impression that they didn't care.

Don't waste all the painstaking work you have done to prepare your business plan. Do at least as much research before making contact with investors as you would before going to see a potential customer. It amazes me how often the entrepreneur sits back at the end of a meeting, satisfied with the way his pitch has gone, relaxing in his chair, and speaks the fatal words, "So tell me, what sort of investments do you make here then?"

Then the smile fixes and fades with the realization that the last two hours were wasted because the firm only invests more money than you want to raise, or has not invested in the sector before, or – worst of all – is an investor in a direct competitor and just took a meeting for whatever useful information could be gleaned from you. Yes, it does happen, and no, venture capital firms will not necessarily sign a non-disclosure agreement, especially in the US.

During the months when you are preparing for fund raising, take the trouble to read the venture capital trade press. Make the time to go to some of the industry conferences that are aimed at bringing investors and companies together. At the very least, study the Vultures' websites, paying attention to the companies backed both by the firm as a whole and by the individuals you are meeting. Be ready for investment decisions made for strange reasons.

You may even want to tweak your business plan in order to make sure that it hits the right spot with a specific investor. In any event, take the initiative. Start off by saying, "I was particularly keen to come to see you because of your investment in Xcorp. It is not a competitor of ours but does share some common characteristics. We might be able to help each other."

A CLOSE SHAVE: AN INVESTMENT DECISION
TAKEN FOR A STRANGE REASON

"I am very sorry, Keith." The young venture capitalist's embarrassment showed in the pink color suffusing his smooth cheeks. "It is an absolutely strict rule of ours. My chairman will not let us make investments in companies run by bearded CEOs. Not in any circumstances. No, don't ask me why. I think it is because of something that happened to him in the past, but I am not totally sure. And the thing is, I am really keen to proceed with the investment. The due diligence is all but done. But I won't be able to get approval unless you do something about the beard."

The CEO thoughtfully rubbed his hirsute chin. He had worn that beard since his student days. He was rather attached to it. What is more, so was his wife.

"Thank you, Keith. You look a new man. And it has been a useful meeting. We've nailed all the outstanding issues, I think." The venture capitalist laughed nervously. "Now I can press on and get approval for the investment."

The CEO rubbed his shaven cheek. His face felt cold.

"I am terribly sorry, Keith." This time the news was delivered over the telephone. "Terribly sorry. The investment committee turned me down. They decided we should not make another investment in this sector."

The CEO put the phone down quickly. He did not like the feel of the receiver against his bare skin.

When you ask questions, ask them in such a way that demonstrates your knowledge, not your ignorance. "Which fund are you investing at the moment?" is not a good question. "I read in the *Venture Capital Journal* that you are raising a new fund. But from the information on your website it was not quite clear whether your previous fund is fully invested or not. Which fund are you investing at the moment?" is a good question.

"What was your background before coming here?" is a bad question. "I see you were at Xsoft before coming here. Did you know Joe Bloggs? I worked with him at his previous place" is a good question. The Vulture will be both flattered that you have taken the time to do your research properly, and impressed that you understand his business and are plugged in.

Doing your research before your first meeting reduces your chances of wasting your time, increases your chances of success, and can also save you time later when you are doing your detailed due diligence before accepting investors' money.

ADVISERS

Is it worth hiring a corporate finance adviser to help you raise money? The answer may well be yes, if you find the right one. To get this book published I had to have an agent. Very few publishers accept proposals directly from authors these days. Indeed, without my agent's encouragement and market awareness I would not have started writing this book in the first place. Thank you, Robert; you have definitely earned your 15%.

Raising investment is slightly different, because you do not have to have an adviser. Ultimately it is you, not your corporate finance adviser, who raises the money. The adviser may give you a leg up and place you in a better position to close the money; but you still have to do the closing.

From the Vulture's perspective there are pros and cons about a deal coming through an adviser. In most cases it is more likely to get through the initial filter than if it is a cold call, although there are a small number of firms that refuse to accept proposals from advisers at all. Nevertheless, most venture firms are happy to build relationships with advisers because they could be the source of other deals in the future. So in the absence of some other contact, having an adviser should increase your chance of getting through the door. It is always easier to say a brusque "no" to someone you have never met.

Another positive for the Vulture of an adviser-introduced deal is that they know that a preliminary filter has been applied. The adviser will normally charge a retainer (which they will describe as modest and you will feel is not), but most of their remuneration comes in a success fee when they raise the money. So they will only take on deals where they think they have a reasonably good chance of success. An adviser's deal should therefore on average be more fundable than a deal off the street.

On the other hand, as I have alluded to before, an adviser should have carefully coached his client and packaged his business plan. The Vulture will have to tear harder to break through the skin of the deal and to reach its flesh. He will also know that he is more likely to be in a competitive position against other Vultures, and that the adviser will be playing one off against the other. Winning the deal will probably be more about pure valuation and less about the softer issues of who will be the best and most constructive investor over a long period.

For the entrepreneur, especially if your company is at an early stage and you are trying to raise a relatively small amount of money, finding an adviser may not be easy. There are fewer advisers who specialize in raising capital than there are investors. And remember the usual rules: validate your short list's track record carefully; find out which investors they really know well; and do some careful reference checking with a random selection of past clients. When your adviser is in place, keep his feet to the fire, and make sure that he is doing all the legwork that you would otherwise have to do yourself, and that you are getting the briefings before meetings that will enable you to ask the good questions, not the bad. After all, that is part of the reason you are paying the adviser his retainer; and it will increase his chance of earning his success fee.

OTHER WAYS IN

If you have your Angel on board before approaching the Vultures, it is likely that the Angel will have a range of useful contacts which may help to make an adviser unnecessary. That, of course, begs the question of how you identify your Angel in the first place. Angels tend to be more ephemeral creatures than Vultures, who can at least be spotted from miles away spiraling down to feed, even if they are sometimes difficult to approach.

Business Angel networks are of course one easy way of contacting Angels. Some of these networks can be akin to advisers in their fee structure, and they are not necessarily the only answer, because a lot of Angels do not join these networks but prefer to find deals through their own contacts.

There is thus no substitute for using your own network of friends, former colleagues, and professional advisers. Look at some businesses which are similar to your own and identify where they raised money. Ring up a few relevant Angel-backed chief executives out of the blue; the worst that can happen is that they refuse to help. Start reading relevant publications and noting down possibly useful contacts well before you plan to raise money. There is a list of helpful resources in the Appendix.

CHOOSING THE INVESTOR

Entrepreneurs should never forget that the process of raising money should be as much about choosing your investor as being chosen by them. When you are being subjected to the overweening arrogance of some venture capital investors it may not seem that way, but that is how it is. Never allow yourself to get into a position where you have no alternative but to take money from one particular investor. Make sure you always have a choice, even if it is only a choice between taking money from a source with which you do not feel comfortable and not raising money at all. Don't ramp up your overhead past the point of no return. Don't ever get yourself into a position where you cannot walk away. It could well be better to close your business down and move on to the next thing than to take money from the wrong investor and waste five years of your life.

Note that I have been talking about the right and wrong investor, not the right or wrong *deal*. Price really should not be the only consideration. In the next two chapters I talk about valuations and the other terms that really matter in the deal. Price is of course a major consideration, but I would rather have an investor I felt totally comfortable with at a lower price than one I was unsure about at a higher. And it is possible to raise money at too high a price because to do so can make future funding rounds difficult or impossible, as well as souring the relationship with your investor (more on this in Chapter 11). After all, what really matters is how successful your company becomes and how much of it you own at the exit, not how much you are left with after the first round.

And in Chapter 6 I come on to what you can realistically expect to get from your investor – the added value they all talk about being able to provide – and how you can best obtain it. Right now, when you are weighing up two term sheets and trying to make a choice, just concentrate on two things. Make sure that you have a personal rapport with the individual who is going to join your board. And check out him, and his firm, carefully with a random selection of entrepreneurs he has backed before.

Whenever I was trying to win a deal I always offered to introduce the entrepreneurs to any of the companies I had previously backed. Most people only made a couple of calls. Some made none. If the roles had been reversed I would have wanted to make more – and as a Vulture I certainly would take up far more than a couple of references on the entrepreneur I was planning to back, or I would not have been doing my job properly. If the entrepreneur took up no references on me I used to feel mildly flattered that my reputation was so strong and my charm so convincing, but underneath my sense of wellbeing a little alarm bell would start ringing; either they are desperate for money, it would warn, or they have a commercial blind spot.

When you do your checking, remember what you are trying to establish. You want your backers to be pleasant to work with. Obviously they must be honest, straightforward, and fair, although you do not want them to be a pushover. You want to hear that they are capable of being firm when necessary. You do not want to hear that they are mindlessly supportive all the time – supportive, yes of course, when backs are to the wall, but clear that sometimes the sensible price for that support is necessary change. So make sure that you talk to some CEOs who have passed through crises with the Vulture you are considering making your own, and even to some of the founders he backed who are no longer CEOs. And remember Chapter 2: ask not just about the individual concerned, but also about his firm and how he is positioned in it, how influential he is, and whether he can normally swing things to his advantage.

CHAPTER FOUR

Valuations and Tricks of the Trade

All the fun of the fair?

The phone rings. You pick up. At the other end you hear the voice you have been hoping for, but also dreading. It drawls, "I've got some good news for you. We've decided to give you a term sheet."

You wave angrily at the two guys who are holding a noisy debate at the water cooler, and hiss under your breath, "Shut up, this is important, I can't hear."

"A term sheet? Wow, that's fantastic. That is great news. What is the valuation?"

Now the water cooler debate stops as its protagonists prick up their ears at that magic phrase "term sheet."

"Valuation? It's 5 million." Did you detect a strange note of reserve at the other end of the phone?

"OK..." you say cautiously.

"Yeah, 5 mill. That's pre-money, on a fully diluted basis, of course. No, sorry, I'm being stupid, I mean post. Post the agreed raise. And that's in headline terms. There is a modest liquidation preference and we'll need to refresh the option pool. But it's pretty much what you were asking for. In the right ball park. In the zone." Nervous laughter. "Of course, there'll be some drawdown milestones, and our standard anti-dilution provisions. We decided we needed some backstop redemption rights, and a bit of a participating dividend. But in the end we came down against a ratchet." Pause and sigh. "Look, you'll need to see the term sheet to really get it. I'll stick it on the email right away."

The email arrives. Breathless with triumphant excitement, you open the treasured attachment and try to read it on the screen. It dances mockingly before your eyes. You blink and rub your head. It's not quite as clear as you thought it would be. Then you decide to print it; after all, you want something you can wave around the office. When you've done your victory dance you sit down in a quiet meeting room to read it more carefully. Then you wrap a cold towel around your aching head.

TERM SHEETS

A term sheet is a document which outlines the terms of the proposed investment in detail. "Term" may be right; "sheet" is perhaps not. It was a very long time ago that I last saw one on a single sheet of paper.

The theory of a term sheet is good. It is meant to flush out all the possible issues which might give rise to later disagreement and fix them before the deal is agreed. Term sheets are not legally binding, except usually a clause agreeing to cover certain professional fees under certain circumstances, a clause giving the investor a period of exclusivity to complete the deal during which the company agrees not to talk to other potential investors, and perhaps a clause agreeing to mutual confidentiality if the deal collapses.

Otherwise there are many let-outs. All term sheets are subject to a number of preconditions such as formal investment committee approval, satisfactory completion of due diligence and reference checking, and completion of contractual documentation to each party's satisfaction. These preconditions are always written loosely enough that in practice the investor can walk away if he wants to. I have never seen data which shows what proportion of term sheets move through to a completed deal, but if it is a majority, it is certainly not a landslide. By the same token, term sheets are also loose enough for the company to walk away, albeit usually at the cost of paying some of the investor's fees. Nevertheless, somehow it doesn't often seem to work like that; normally, if anyone walks away it's the investor.

In spite of the fact that term sheets are by and large non-binding, their complexity nowadays is such that lawyers on both sides often get involved in reviewing them. So in spite of the theoretical benefit of a term sheet – namely, that most of the detail will have been thrashed out in advance – in practice it can simply mean that you have two protracted negotiations, one over the term sheet, and another over the substantive contractual documentation.

Many entrepreneurs have returned to their offices waving term sheets in triumph, like Neville Chamberlain returning from Munich, only to have their hopes shattered in subsequent weeks when the deal fails to stick. For all that, a term sheet is an important step forward, because although it is not legally binding, a venture firm cannot afford to get a reputation for tossing term sheets around like confetti and then regularly failing to follow through with them.

SIMPLE VALUATIONS

Term sheets have become steadily longer over the years. The main reason is that deal structures have become ever more complicated. I view myself as an optimistic progressive, so terms like "in the good old days" do not really come naturally to me, but here I cannot prevent myself.

In the good old days, if an investor offered $1 million for 25% of the equity, it generally meant what it said. Until that moment, as there is no market in your shares, there is no empirical way of calculating your company's value. But, you might think, once the investment offer is made, the valuation should be pretty easy to calculate. If the investor puts down $1 million for one quarter of the business, then surely the business is worth $4 million. You simply divide the amount being invested by the proportion of the equity it buys, in this example

$1 million divided by 25%. On a simple "post-money" basis at least, that is easy and correct.

Another way of deriving the valuation is to look at the price per share. Say your company has three million shares in issue before the investment takes place. Then your investor pays $1 million for one million new shares at $1 each. Now you have four million shares in issue, on which your new investor's deal has placed a price of $1 each. You are back at the $4 million valuation again. This is the same basic methodology used for calculating the "market capitalization" of quoted companies – the number of shares in issue multiplied by the prevailing share price. The post-money valuation, or the price per share, is also referred to as the investor's "entry valuation," "entry capitalization," or "entry price." See the column headed "post-money valuation (1)" in the table opposite.

But what if your investor has put not just $1 million but $2 million into the business at the same $1 price per share? Then, after the investment, there would be five million shares in issue, and your investor would own two million of them, equivalent to a stake of 40%. The post-money valuation is $1 million higher, but your equity stake, at 60% instead of 75% (assuming you owned the whole business before the investment was made), is 15 percentage points lower. 15 percentage points lower (75 minus 60), please note, but 20 *percent* lower (15 over 75). See the column headed "post-money valuation (2)" in the table.

However, the "pre-money valuation" is the same in each case. This is calculated by subtracting the amount invested from the post-money valuation (or by multiplying the shares in issue before investment by the price per share), so in both these examples the pre-money valuation – "pre-money" for short, or even "pre" for shorter – is $3 million. All other things being equal, a higher pre-money valuation will mean that you have sold less of your business; but a higher post-money may mean that you have sold a higher proportion of it.

I hope the table makes things clearer.

		Pre-money valuation	Post-money valuation (1)	Post-money valuation (2)	Formulae
Amount raised	A	–	$1,000,000	$2,000,000	(BxD), (I–H)
Price per share	B	Unfixed	$1	$1	(A/D)
Old shares in issue	C	3,000,000	3,000,000	3,000,000	
New shares issued	D	–	1,000,000	2,000,000	(A/B)
New total shares	E	–	4,000,000	5,000,000	(C+D)
Management ownership	F	100%	75%	60%	(100%–G)
Investor ownership	G	–	25%	40%	(D/C)%, (A/I)%
Pre-money valuation	H	Unfixed	$3,000,000	$3,000,000	(BxC), (I–A)
Post-money valuation	I	Unfixed	$4,000,000	$5,000,000	(A+H), (BxE), (A/G)

Another concept related to this is the "enterprise valuation." The enterprise valuation, or inevitably EV for short, is the market capitalization of a business (the number of shares in issue times the share price) after any spare cash has been deducted, or any debt added. The theory here is that the underlying business has a certain intrinsic value and, if it is sold, any excess cash increases the value, whereas any debt has to be repaid and decreases the value.

So immediately after your venture capital investment has taken place, your enterprise valuation and your pre-money valuation are theoretically the same. $1 million has gone in for 25% of the equity, giving you a post-money valuation of $4 million, a pre-money of $3 million, and an enterprise value of $3 million (4 million shares times $1 dollar, minus $1 million in spare cash).

But what happens six months later when you've spent half that cash? As you're a private company, there's no method of calculating your share price from day to day, so no change can be discerned in the post-money valuation. There are still 4 million shares in issue, and the last price paid for those shares was $1 each. However, it can be argued that your enterprise value is now theoretically $3.5 million – your $4 million post-money valuation, less the $0.5 million you have left in cash. Maybe you did spend that cash in such a way as to increase the value of the business by precisely $0.5 million. If you haven't used it to increase the value of the underlying business – the enterprise value – by $0.5 million, then the real value per share – the only other variable in the equation – must have gone down.

Making the same point in tabular form:

		Immediately after investment	Six months later	Formulae
Shares in issue	A	4,000,000	4,000,000	
Price per share	B	$1	$1	
Post-money valuation	C	$4,000,000	$4,000,000	(AxB)
Cash at bank	D	$1,000,000	$500,000	
Enterprise value	E	$3,000,000	$3,500,000	(C–D)

In reality in a private company you cannot confirm this calculation unless you sell the business, or until you sell more shares in it. You and your investor will hope that you have spent the $0.5 million very wisely and increased the enterprise value by more than has been invested; but maybe you have wasted it.

I am laboring this point to demonstrate that there are already a number of different ways of looking at the valuation of your business. You have a post-money valuation, a pre-money valuation, and an enterprise valuation. After six months, some may be different. And that is after the simplest of possible deals. What is more, you have already faced one decision which may have had a major impact on your wealth. Did you decide back there to raise $1 million, or did you raise $2 million? Did you keep 75% of the company, or 60%? Will you need $2 million to grow the business as you want? If you are going to need that much, could you make do with $1 million now and raise a second $1 million later at a higher price per share, or a higher pre-money? Are you confident enough to take the risk that you might not be able to raise the second $1 million later, because your progress has been poor, or because the investment climate has changed for the worse?

IT GETS MORE COMPLICATED... WITH DOWNSIDE PROTECTION

In any case, we do not live in the good old days, we live in the present. And in the present you are unlikely to get a simple, straightforward, ordinary share deal, from a Vulture at least. You are more likely, for the reasons explained later, to get it from an Angel or a Dragon, but even here some additional complexity is possible.

Let's look at it from the Vulture's point of view, for once. Say they do invest in common stock, in ordinary shares, just like yours, at the $4 million price. Say things do not progress quite how you and they want, and a couple of years down the track you decide to sell the business for $2 million. You still own 75% of it, remember, so you bank $1.5 million. It's not as much as you'd hoped for, but as you put in next to no cash, it's a lot better than a poke in the eye with a sharp stick. Your Vulture, though, loses half his money and his feathers start falling out at the injustice of it all. "Why should you make a decent chunk of change," he asks with resentment, "when we're losing half our money?"

So the next time he does a deal, he introduces some downside protection.

Downside protection comes in many shapes and sizes. The most benign form is often referred to as "premium retrieval." This means that if the business is sold at a lower valuation than the post-money entry valuation, the investor will have the right to get back the price he paid – the "premium" he paid for his shares – before the other shareholders – that is, you – get anything. In the US this structure is normally achieved by investors buying Preferred Shares which, at their option, either get repaid or convert into Common Stock. So in circumstances where the Common Stock will be worth more than the Preferred Shares' cost they convert, otherwise they redeem. In the UK this same mechanism may be used, or premium retrieval rights are written into the Articles of Association.

Let's stick with our original example – $1 million in for 25% – and understand the implications of this new rule.

Now, if the business is sold for $1 million or less, the Vulture gets everything, and you get nothing. This is the amount invested by the Vulture, the "share premium" he has paid, or the price of his Preferred Shares. You then get all the proceeds between $1 million and $4 million, the post-money valuation. At the post-money valuation, the division of the proceeds comes back into sync with the equity percentages because you have 75% to the Vulture's 25%. It continues in that proportion ever upward.

What is effectively happening here is that the percentage ownership of the business is shifting according to the sale price. In one sense, the investor's entry valuation diminishes if the exit price reduces. In the event that the business is sold for $1.5 million, the investor's post-money valuation is that $1.5 million, and the pre-money only $0.5 million. But that is contingent on a future unknown event.

One of the strange results of this type of deal structure is that the investor doesn't really care whether the company is sold for $1 million or $4 million. Either way he gets $1 million. You care a lot, because it's the difference between a big fat zero and $3 million. But you don't care whether the company is sold for $1 million or $0.5 million, because below $1 million everything goes toward paying back the investor's cost – so why should you bother? In practice perhaps the investor may have to offer you some incentive to cooperate with the sale (more on this topic in Chapter 12 on exits).

The next table (overleaf) shows the impact of a simple Preferred Share or premium retrieval on the distribution of the proceeds at different exit valuations.

AND THEN IT GETS MORE COMPLICATED STILL... WITH A LIQUIDATION PREFERENCE

If you've switched off, I can only apologize. I'm being as clear as I know how. There's a graph toward the end of this chapter which compares how all these different deal structures work at different exit prices; that may help. But now's the moment to switch back on again, because most investments nowadays are structured with a liquidation preference, and that's what I'm going to attempt to explain next.

Let's get back into the Vultures' nest. Those feathers are still falling out and they're getting balder and balder, because you've just sold the company for $3 million. They've got their money

Distribution of proceeds with simple Preference Share or premium retrieval.

Exit price	A	At invest-ment	$1 million	$2 million	$3 million	$4 million	$5 million	Formula
Amount invested	B	$1,000,000	$1,000,000	$1,000,000	$1,000,000	$1,000,000	$1,000,000	
Investor proceeds	C		$1,000,000	$1,000,000	$1,000,000	$1,000,000	$1,250,000	>B or (A x 25%)
Investor %	D	25%	100%	50%	33%	25%	25%	C/A
Management proceeds	E		$0	$1,000,000	$2,000,000	$3,000,000	$3,750,000	A–C
Management %	F	75%	0%	50%	67%	75%	75%	E/A
Effective post-money valuation	G	$4,000,000	$1,000,000	$2,000,000	$3,000,000	$4,000,000	$5,000,000	B/D
Effective pre-money valuation	H	$3,000,000	$0	$1,000,000	$2,000,000	$3,000,000	$4,000,000	(B/D) – B

back thanks to their premium retrieval, so it's better than nothing. But you've banked a $2 million profit (see the fourth column from the right in the table above). Surely the Vultures deserve some sort of positive return on their investment? You can't expect them just to sit there and get no return at all after five years.

So, instead of investing in straightforward Preferred Shares or ordinary shares with premium retrieval, the Vultures invest in Series A Preferred Participating Shares. These have the right to be paid back in full first (the Preferred bit), and then to get their equity percentage at any exit valuation if there's anything left (the Participating bit). So, at an exit price of $1 million or below, the position's the same as with premium retrieval; everything goes to your Vultures. But at $2 million, they get their $1 million cost plus their 25% share of the remaining $1 million. That's $1.25 million in total. And at $4 million, the post-money entry capitalization, they get $1.75 million ($1 million cost, plus 25% of $4 million minus $1 million).

Here's the table adjusted for a full liquidation preference.

Exit price	A	At invest-ment	$1 million	$2 million	$3 million	$4 million	$5 million	Formula
Amount invested	B	$1,000,000	$1,000,000	$1,000,000	$1,000,000	$1,000,000	$1,000,000	
Investor proceeds	C		$1,000,000	$1,250,000	$1,500,000	$1,750,000	$2,000,000	B+(A–B) x 25%
Investor %	D	25%	100%	62.5%	50%	43.75%	40%	C/A
Management proceeds	E		$0	$750,000	$1,500,000	$2,250,000	$3,000,000	A–C
Management %	F	75%	0%	37.5%	50%	56.25%	60%	E/A
Effective post-money valuation	G	$4,000,000	$1,000,000	$1,600,000	$2,000,000	$2,286,000	$2,500,000	B/D
Effective pre-money valuation	H	$3,000,000	$0	$600,000	$1,000,000	$1,286,000	$1,500,000	G – B

Hang on a moment. Let me look at that table more closely. Are those numbers in the $4 million exit price column right? That means...

Yes, that means that the post-money entry capitalization was not really $4 million at all. It was $2.286 million. And if the post-money was $2.286 million, and $1 million went in, the pre-money must have been... $1.286 million. So the effect of simply changing the investment instrument has been to reduce the value attaching to the existing business by two-thirds. Hmm.

I bet you have your calculator out now and are checking my math. You've done the sum twice? Yes, you are doing it right. Have you satisfied your incredulity? If you divide the amount the investor put in – $1 million – by their share of the proceeds at a $4 million exit price – 43.75% – the answer really is $2.286 million. Or $2,285,714 if you want to be pedantic.

But you're certain someone said that the post-money valuation was $4 million. You look back at the term sheet. Look, it's there, right at the top of the term sheet. $1 million has gone into the company for 25% of the equity, so the valuation is $4 million. That is known as the "headline" valuation, but it's not necessarily the real valuation at all.

If you go on to make a huge success of your business and sell it for $100 million, the $1 million liquidation preference pales into relative insignificance. It becomes 1% of the total proceeds, so that the investor gets about 26% and you get 74%. You may not bother to quibble about that too much; it's close enough to the 25/75 split implied in the term sheet. But if modest success is achieved, say a $10 million exit, the effect of the liquidation preference is to take the investor up to 32.5% of the proceeds or $3.25 million ($10 million minus $1 million times 25% plus $1 million). That's 7.5 percentage points higher than implied by the headline equity split, or fully 30% better. And at the lower end, as the table on the previous page makes clear, the impact is even more striking.

Now, to paraphrase something more important, the Vulture saw that the liquidation preference was good. So the Vulture said, "Let there be a two times liquidation preference." This means that the Series A Preferred Participating Shares are entitled to not just their cost before any other class of share, but to twice their cost. Look at the impact of that:

Exit price	A	At investment	$1 million	$2 million	$3 million	$4 million	$5 million	Formula
Amount invested	B	$1,000,000	$1,000,000	$1,000,000	$1,000,000	$1,000,000	$1,000,000	
Investor proceeds	C		$1,000,000	$2,000,000	$2,250,000	$2,500,000	$2,750,000	B + (A–B) x 25%
Investor %	D	25%	100%	100%	75%	62.5%	55%	C/A
Management proceeds	E		$0	$0	$750,000	$1,500,000	$3,750,000	A–C
Management %	F	75%	0% .	0%	25%	37.5%	45%	E/A
Effective post-money valuation	G	$4,000,000	$1,000,000	$1,000,000	$1,333,333	$1,600,000	$1,818,181	B/D
Effective pre-money valuation	H	$3,000,000	$0	$0	$333,333	$600,000	$818,181	G – B

Now, at an exit at that headline valuation of $4 million, the effective pre-money valuation is just $0.6 million – only 20%

of the pre-money apparently implied by the investment of $1 million for 25%. I always say that you shouldn't believe what you read in the headlines.

So it is clear that the Series A Preferred Participating Share mechanism does a little bit more than just give the Vulture downside protection; it enhances his returns (and reduces yours) very significantly in those middle-ranking (and therefore quite probable) outcomes. The Vulture may not be soaring as high on those thermals as he really likes, but he's well up into the air at least.

The psychology of the liquidation preference largely depends on the incurable optimism of the entrepreneur. The upside beckons. Failure, or even a merely modest success, is unthinkable.

Anyway, nowadays a one times liquidation preference is a fairly standard feature of venture capital investment. Multiple liquidation preferences are less common, especially in the first round. You may well have to accept Preferred Preference Shares and the liquidation preference implied by them in your deal. Just make sure that you understand the implications in full.

A FEW MORE BELLS AND WHISTLES (OR BILLS AND WHISTLING?)

But that isn't all. Let's go back to the $10 million exit price we used a couple of pages ago. With the benefit of his simple one times liquidation preference, that gave the Vulture $3.25 million out of $10 million – a 3.25 times return on his $1 million investment. After five years that works out at an internal rate of return of 26.6%. That could be worse, but it's not as high as the base case he targeted on the investment (remember Chapter 2?).

"I needed an IRR with a '3' at the front of it at least. That," says the Vulture, "is why I included in the term sheet the right to a 10% fixed annual dividend on the Series A Preferred Stock. That gives me another $850K."

"$850K?" you say, with worried surprise in your voice. "10% on $1 million is $100,000. Its only been five years – it may seem longer – but that's $500,000, surely."

"Nawh. It's cumulative. It compounds annually. So it is $850K. Do the math. So in total I am now getting $4.1 million."

Now you really choke. That is a bill that makes you whistle. "But that's 41% of the total proceeds; you're only meant to have 25% of the company."

"At least we managed to sell the business, so that you didn't have to find the $1.85 million it would have cost you to redeem the Series A Prefs plus the dividend. That was my backstop in case we were unable to achieve a full equity exit."

Hmm, you think. Perhaps I would have been better off to redeem the Prefs and then sell the business later.

AND MORE COMPLICATED STILL... WITH SOME LOAN NOTES

Under the terms of the Shareholders' Agreement or Investor Rights Agreement you would not be able to do that without the Vulture's consent (more on that subject in the next chapter), but to remove any thought of that temptation from you, deals are sometimes structured with a small investment in ordinary equity and the balance in Redeemable Preference Shares or Loan Notes. This then places two different types of valuation on the business: the "equity capitalization" and the "risk capitalization."

Say that 10% of the $1 million is invested in equity shares, and 90% in Loan Notes, still for 25% of the equity. Now you have an equity capitalization of just $0.4 million ($100,000/25%). Your risk capitalization is still $4 million ($1 million/25%), except that now your company has a debt of

$0.9 million. Because that has to be repaid at some point it should really be deducted to give a post-money risk capitalization of $3.1 million. And if the Loan Notes have a right to interest, as they probably will, then doesn't that really mean that the equity valuation goes down as the interest payable builds up and eats into the value attributable to the shares?

Here's another table to make it clear. I have assumed here that the Loan Notes accumulate compound interest at 10% per annum and that there is no movement from $4 million in the underlying value of the business.

		Investment	Year 1	Year 3	Year 5	Formula
Total investment	A	$1,000,000				
Equity cost	B	$100,000				
Equity capitalization	C	$400,000				B/F
Original risk capitalization	D	$4,000,000				A/G
Cumulative interest	E	10% p.a.	$90,000	$298,000	$549,000	
Loan stock plus interest	F	$900,000	$990,000	$1,198,000	$1,449,000	
Effective investor equity	G	25%	27.25%	32.45%	38.74%	(B+F)/D
Effective risk capitalization	H	$4,000,000	$3,670,000	$3,082,000	$2,581,000	D/G

So at a $4 million exit valuation, the Vulture's take climbs from 25% when the deal is done to 38.74% by Year 5. Or if you prefer to look at it the other way round, the post-money risk capitalization reduces from $4 million to $2.581 million just as a result of the cumulative interest on the Loan Notes element.

Occasionally I've seen deals where all the investment is made in Loan Notes. I see your ears prick up. Isn't that better, because no equity's been given away? Ah. I forgot to say that in those circumstances the Loan Notes come with conversion rights into the equity or with low-priced warrants attached to them.

In our example of the $1 million investment for 25% of the company, if the investment took place all in Convertible Loan Notes, the post-money risk capitalization remains the same – $4 million – but because no money at all is being invested in shares, no equity capitalization can really be calculated. This structure has a very similar effect to an investment in non-participating Series A Preferred Shares, with two provisos. It is easier for the investor to get Loan Notes repaid, partly because they may be secured, and partly because they can be repaid before the company has accumulated profits, whereas Preference Shares can generally only be redeemed out of accu-mulated profits. And because of this, having Loan Notes makes your balance sheet look weaker and may make customer and supplier interactions more troublesome.

If the Loan Notes are not convertible but have low-priced warrants attached to them, the effect is to all intents and pur-poses the same as a Series A Participating Preferred deal (except for the balance sheet consideration). At an exit below $1 million plus accumulated interest or dividends, all the pro-ceeds go to the Loan Stock holders, and it makes no difference whether they exercise their warrants or not. Above $1 million, they exercise the warrants and take their 25% equity percent-age on top of their Loan Stock repayment, just like the Series A Participating Prefs.

SHE WONDERS HOW IT EVER GOT THIS CRAZY

That, of course, is a line from the great Eagles song "Lying Eyes." It may be unfair to apply an Eagles song to Vultures, perhaps, even if the title sounds as if it might be about venture capital. Certainly many truly crazy things happened during the internet bubble in 1999 and 2000. One of these was that some entrepreneurs became utterly fixated on the headline valuations that investors were placing on their companies. Failure was even more inconceivable than usual; only the upside mattered. The higher the headline post-money valuation, the cooler, the more macho, and the more desirable you became. You could boast in bars about how much money you were worth – on paper. Some venture capital investors reacted to this idiocy equally idiotically with increased levels of liquidation preference.

"So you want a $100 million post-money valuation? Sure, sure, given you've already got $0.5 million of revenue, that's totally justified. We'll put in $20 million for 20%. We'll need a 4× liquidation preference, but with your massive no-lose upside potential that shouldn't give you a problem."

So in spite of the headline valuation of $100 million, at an exit valuation of $100 million, with this deal the investor would receive $84 million (the liquidation preference of 4× $20 million ($80 million) plus 20% of the remaining $20 million). With no change from the headline valuation of $100 million, the other shareholders would actually just get $16 million for their theoretical 80% equity share. And if the exit value was only $80 million, they would get nothing at all while the investors made four times their money. Stories are told of deals that were structured with liquidation preferences of 10×.

Those crazy days, thank heavens, have gone. One of the lessons that have been learned, or relearned, by many in the industry is that simple deals have considerable merits, not least because everyone can remember where they stand, interests are aligned, and motivation persists.

ARE ANGELS AND DRAGONS NICER THAN VULTURES?

Partly because Angels and Dragons may have been on the receiving end of a complex Vulture-structured deal in the days when they were entrepreneurs, they are more likely to favor simple deals. They may have felt the demoralizing impact that an overcomplicated deal structure can have. You may even find that they are willing to forgo the downside protection afforded by a Preferred Share with a simple liquidation preference.

Before you jump to the conclusion that these private investors are necessarily more generous than their institutional cousins, remember that some tax authorities give generous incentives for investment in private companies – provided that the investment is made in Common Stock or ordinary shares. This applies under the Enterprise Investment Scheme in the UK, for example. Angels or Dragons may therefore prefer to take ordinary shares with premium retrieval but less protection than Participating Preferred Shares and reduce their tax bill.

And I wouldn't count on them not driving a harder bargain on the equity percentage in return for offering a plain vanilla equity deal. It's called enlightened self-interest.

OTHER THINGS THAT GO BUMP IN THE NIGHT AND AFFECT VALUATION

I hope you now understand the horrible complications implicit in the front page of that term sheet that you were waving in triumph a little while ago. You turn to page 2, or page 3, or page 11. Surely it all gets simpler?

Maybe you've had enough. Look at it again in the morning. But there are still things there which may have a huge impact on the valuation placed on your equity by the term sheet in different exit circumstances. Here are some of them.

Options

Options, of course, are a good thing. They are there to motivate management. So you cast a cursory but positive eye over the term sheet clause which alludes to an option pool of 15%. Good.

Wait a moment. From whose equity does that 15% come? Doesn't the way it is worded imply 15% of the expanded equity before the investment takes place? So, looking at things on a fully diluted equity basis after the new investment, that means 15% for the option pool and 25% for the new investor, which adds up to 40%. That only leaves 60% for you. Wasn't the deal meant to be 25% for the investor and 75% for you? Surely the 15% for the option pool should be on top of that 1:3 ratio, so that when all the options are granted you go down to 63.75% but the investor goes down by the same proportion to 21.25%?

Just check that your investor hasn't managed to chisel another 3.75 percentage points away from you. It may not sound a lot, expressed like that, but the useful table below shows that it can make a big difference in the notional value of your stake of 25%.

	Options allocated before investment	Options allocated after investment	Difference
Amount invested	$1,000,000	$1,000,000	–
Investor	25%	21.25%	–15%
Management	60%	63.75%	+6.25%
Options	15%	15%	–
Fully diluted post-money	$4,000,000	$4,705,000	+15%
Notional value of management stake	$2,400,000	$3,000,000	+25%

Anti-dilution

"Anti-dilution, eh? Well, I'm with you there, Vulture. I am anti-dilution in principle. But surely you are not anti-dilution. You are the one who is causing me dilution. So why have you got an anti-dilution clause in your term sheet?"

Your prospective Vulture shuffles his claws uncomfortably. Just read it again, more slowly this time, he says. You read it again.

"OK, I think I understand now. If we have to raise another round of funding, and can only do so at a lower price, then you get more shares so that your overall price goes down to the same price as that next round. So tell me, Vulture, why is that fair? Effectively you want an option to reduce the price paid if future events demonstrate that you were wrong to pay the price you are now proposing. You don't normally get that protection if you buy shares in a company."

"Ah," says the Vulture, "but the price I'm paying is not based on the value of your company today. I'm paying a much higher price than your company's really worth today. It's a discounted price based on what the company might be worth in the future. So it's only fair for me to have anti-dilution rights."

The Vulture, you soon find, however eloquently you argue, is irrevocably stapled to these anti-dilution rights. This is perhaps because in recent years he has seen new investors coming in after him, at a lower price, taking a lower risk, and getting an exit in a shorter space of time. That means that the later-stage investor is giving his customers a far better return for a lower risk. No prizes for guessing which Vulture will most easily be able to raise his next fund.

Because of the frequency in recent years of later rounds taking place at lower prices than earlier rounds, and the concomitant negative impact on early-stage investors, you may find that in order to raise money you have no choice but to grant certain anti-dilution rights. I have alluded to these so-called down rounds before and will talk about them and the other intricacies of follow-on rounds in full in Chapter 11. But because you may have to give anti-dilution rights in your first round in anticipation of future rounds, and because they can have a major impact on your real first-round valuation, I need to deal with the theory here.

How do they work? Let's go back to our tried-and-tested example. There are 4 million shares in issue after your first round. The exemplary investor paid $1 each for 1 million of them. Say we need to raise some more money, and say we find a new investor who's willing to put in another $1 million. That is the good news; the bad news is that he will only pay a post-money valuation of $3 million, or $2 million pre. That means the new investor needs one third of the expanded equity, or 2 million shares (2 million/6 million = 33.3%). So the share price implied by the new investor's proposal is 50 cents ($1 million/2 million shares).

Without anti-dilution rights, the new investor would be getting twice as good a deal as the first investor. Your original investor and you would be diluted by one third each, as follows.

	Management shares	%	Investor 1	Price	%	Investor 2	Price	%
Original round	3,000,000	75%	1,000,000	$1	25%	–	–	–
Original post-money			$4,000,000					
Original pre-money			$3,000,000					
New round	3,000,000	50%	1,000,000	$1	16.7%	2,000,000	$0.50	33.3%
New post-money			$6,000,000			$3,000,000		
New pre-money			$4,000,000			$2,000,000		

However, full anti-dilution rights entitle your first investor to get the same price per share as the new investor. So that triggers another 1 million shares for the old investor, to get his effective price down to the 50 cents being paid by the new investor. Unfortunately, now there are 5 million shares in issue attributable to the old shareholders before the new investment. The new investor still wants one third of the company to get his pre-money of $2 million and his post-money of $3 million. So now he needs 2.5 million shares (2.5 million/7.5 million = 33.3%). That means that his price has to go down again to 40 cents, being $1 million/2.5 million.

But wait a moment. Now investor number one's anti-dilution formula triggers again because he needs to get down to 40 cents per share. That gives him another 500,000 shares. And that means the new investor has to have more shares, and a lower price, which triggers another iteration. In this example the iterations end with the share price at 33.3 cents, the new investor at 33.3%, the old investor at 33.3%, and you at 33.3%. So as a result of the anti-dilution provision your equity percentage has more than halved. You have also lost control of your company. The pre-money valuation has dropped from a respectable $3 million to a miserable $1 million, reducing the theoretical value of your stake to a third of its previous level.

It may be easier to follow in the next table, overleaf. This is what is known as "full ratchet" anti-dilution protection. You could be excused for thinking that there's little difference between a full ratchet and a thumbscrew. It takes no account of the amount of new money being raised, and theoretically could be triggered by the issue of just one new share at a lower price.

Many now view "full ratchet" anti-dilution as draconian. For this reason, incoming investors may make it a condition of their participation in a second round that the first investor waives some of his full ratchet anti-dilution rights. The new investors may be concerned about the impact on the

Effect of full ratchet anti-dilution warrants

	Management	%	Investor 1	Price	%	Investor 2	Price	%
Original round	3,000,000	75%	1,000,000	$1	25%	–	–	–
Original post-money	$4,000,000		$4,000,000					
Original pre-money	$3,000,000		$3,000,000					
Iteration 1								
New shares			1,000,000			2,000,000	$0.50	
New total	3,000,000	42.9%	2,000,000	$0.50	28.6%	2,000,000	$0.50	28.6%
Iteration 2								
New shares			500,000			500,000		
New total	3,000,000	38.4%	2,500,000	$0.40	31.3%	2,500,000	$0.40	31.3%
Iteration 3								
New shares			500,000			500,000		
New total	3,000,000	33.3%	3,000,000	$0.33	33.3%	3,000,000	$0.33	33/3%
Total investment			$1,000,000			$1,000,000		
New post-money			$3,000,000			$3,000,000		
New pre-money			$1,000,000			$1,000,000		

management team's motivation (more on the subject of incoming investors' concerns about the management team in Chapter 11, you'll be pleased to hear). Because of the difficulty of making full ratchet anti-dilution stick, "weighted average" anti-dilution formulae have become more common. These are somewhat more benign formulae which have regard to the amount of money raised at the old and the new price. They come in two flavors, broad based and narrow based.

Let's do narrow based first. The same basic principles apply and the same iterative process takes place as in the full ratchet example, but the new share price at each point is calculated according to the following weighted average formula:

$$\frac{(\text{Investor 1 amount} + \text{Investor 2 amount})}{(\text{Investor 1 shares} + \text{Investor 2 shares})}$$

In our example the iterations look like the table below.

	Management	%	Investor 1	Price	%	Investor 2	Price	%
Original round	3,000,000	75%	1,000,000	$1	25%	–	–	–
Original post-money	$4,000,000		$4,000,000					
Original pre-money	$3,000,000		$3,000,000					
Iteration 1								
New shares			500,000			2,000,000	$0.50	
New total	3,000,000	46.2%	1,500,000	$0.67	23.1%	2,000,000	$0.50	30.7%
Iteration 2								
New shares			375,000			250,000		
New total	3,000,000	42.1%	1,875,000	$0.53	26.3%	2,250,000	$0.44	31.6%
Iteration 3								
New shares			281,250			187,500		
New total	3,000,000	39.5%	2,156,250	$0.46	28.4%	2,437,500	$0.41	32.1%
Iteration 4								
New shares			140,625			210,938		
New total	3,000,000	37.7%	2,296,875	$0.44	28.9%	2,648,438	$0.38	33.3%
Total investment			$1,000,000			$1,000,000		
New post-money			$3,460,207			$3,000,000		
New pre-money			$2,460,207			$2,000,000		

The relative position of Investor 2 is, of course, unchanged. He offered to invest $1 million for one third of the company, and even though he ends up with fewer shares at a higher price that percentage is what he gets, because there are fewer shares in issue. The positions of the management and Investor 1 are different, though, with the management retaining 37.7% instead of 33.3% under the full ratchet mechanism, and Investor 1 slipping to 28.9%.

Under the broad-based weighted average, you take into account all the shares in issue, not just those held by Investor 1. The weighted average formula is:

$$\frac{\text{(All original shares at Investor 1 price + Investor 2 amount)}}{\text{(All original shares + Investor 1 shares + Investor 2 shares)}}$$

In our example, that works out as in the table opposite.

So the broad-based formula produces a much worse result for the first-round investor, and therefore a much better result for the management shareholders. Once again, the position of the new investor is unaffected.

And what are the implications of all this for valuation, for that is what this chapter is about? In each case the effect is to adjust your valuation downward from the position you would be in without giving your first investors any anti-dilution rights. The full ratchet formula will always be the worst for you, and the broad-based weighted average the best, with the narrow-based weighted average somewhere in between. Of course, because the anti-dilution rights are contingent on a future event, you cannot quantify their impact on valuation up front. All you can do is be aware that they can be highly significant. Perhaps you should have decided to take that full $2 million investment up front instead of splitting it into two rounds of $1 million.

	Management	%	Investor 1	Price	%	Investor 2	Price	%
Original round	3,000,000	75%	1,000,000	$1	25%	–	–	–
Original post-money	$4,000,000		$4,000,000					
Original pre-money	$3,000,000		$3,000,000					
Iteration 1								
New shares			200,000			2,000,000	$0.50	
New total	3,000,000	48.4%	1,200,000	$0.83	19.4%	2,000,000	$0.50	32.2%
Iteration 2								
New shares			60,000			100,000		
New total	3,000,000	47.2%	1,260,000	$0.79	19.8%	2,100,000	$0.48	33.0%
Iteration 3								
New shares			18,000			30,000		
New total	3,000,000	46.9%	1,278,000	$0.78	19.9%	2,130,000	$0.47	33.2%
Iteration 4								
New shares			5,400			11,700		
New total	3,000,000	46.7%	1,283,400	$0.78	20.0%	2,141,700	$0.47	33.3%
Total investment			$1,000,000			$1,000,000		
New post-money			$5,000,000			$3,000,000		
New pre-money			$3,000,000			$2,000,000		

Milestones

From Chapter 2 you may remember the "just-in-time" draw-down structure used by many limited partnership funds to make the Vulture's all-important internal rate of return look as good as possible.

Now, let's say you have decided to raise $2 million up front. You did not much like the risk of having to raise money later, and triggering the term sheet's ferocious anti-dilution provisions. But your prospective Vulture can see that you will not need the second $1 million for a year, or perhaps, if things go well, ever.

So the Vulture suggests that the investment should be staggered. $1 million will be invested on Day 1. $1 million will be available for drawdown, at the company's option, 12 months later. That way the Vulture can delay drawing the second $1 million from his own investors until it is really needed.

That, on its own, seems innocuous enough. Perhaps you could even secure a provision that enables you to claw back some equity if the Vulture defaults for some reason and is unable to fulfill his commitment to make the subsequent investment.

But then the Vulture decides to attach some conditions to the second drawdown. Sometimes the argument can go as follows.

"But in the unlikely event that things have gone a long way off track, I really cannot be expected to put in the second tranche just like that. Certainly not on the same terms, anyway. I'd be failing in my duty to my investors. Let's have some milestones, perhaps linked to the new product development program, to winning a couple of major customers, and to revenue being within 10% of goal."

"Hang on a moment," you might think, "he was the one who asked for tranched drawdowns in the first place. Now he's trying to attach performance conditions to them!"

Sometimes the conversation about milestones is more straightforward and you arrive at the same place by a more direct route.

The Vulture owns up: "I don't feel certain enough about the plan to put the whole $2 million in up front. I'll invest $1 million up front at the valuation we've agreed. You can draw down the next $1 million on the same terms subject to hitting the new product development program, to winning a couple of major customers, and to revenue being within 10% of goal."

Occasionally I have seen milestone-linked deals where the first tranche consists of all the equity that the investor intends to invest, with the second and subsequent tranches coming in as loan stock or another non-equity instrument. This is really a bit of a try-on, because the investor is securing all his equity stake and thus the majority of his upside at the beginning for a smaller outlay. More often, though, each tranche of the investment is structured in the same mix of instruments and priced the same. So a milestone-based deal can have the superficial attraction for the entrepreneur that it limits his initial dilution.

Say that you have been unable to make up your mind whether to raise $1 million or $2 million. Let's still stick to the very first example we used, with a pre-money valuation of $3 million. If you remember, raising $1 million left you and the other original shareholders with 75%; raising $2 million reduced your stake by another 20% (15 percentage points) to 60%. *Prima facie*, getting by with raising a smaller amount is better. So let's get an investor to commit to invest the second tranche. Then we can draw it if we need it, but not if we don't. We don't have to worry about going to a new investor for our second $1 million and running the risk of triggering those nasty anti-dilution warrants.

Unfortunately, things don't often work like that. First of all, many investors will insist on having the right to invest the second tranche if they want to. So if things are going really well, the full amount of money's likely to come in whether you need it or not, causing the maximum amount of dilution.

Secondly, even if you can avoid giving the investor the right to invest – giving what is effectively a one-way "put option" – the chances are that the milestones will mean that you are unable to access the money if you really need it, namely when things have gone worse than planned. If you miss the milestones but need the funding, you are either back where you started, with the need to find a second investor, running the risk of triggering the anti-dilution provisions; or you have to throw yourself on the mercy of your existing investor. Of course, he will most likely say that he has to renegotiate the terms for the rest of the investment because you have missed the milestones and are behind plan. The milestone structure makes it more likely that you will have to bite your lip and accept his terms, because of themselves they make it very clear to other potential new investors that you have underperformed, and thus make your company look a less attractive investment.

The final problem with milestones is that they can lock a company into a particular course. Perhaps the greatest advantage that small businesses have over large ones is that they are more agile and flexible and can adapt their plans more quickly. If you are locked into a particular plan in order to secure your next tranche of funding, it can mean that you have sacrificed your precious flexibility and pursue the wrong strategy for too long.

So what does a milestone deal mean for the valuation the term sheet places on your company? Well, it means that the valuation might be as intended; or it might not. If not, the likelihood is that it will be lower. No wonder this type of deal has become popular with Vultures.

Ratchets

Not ratchets again, please no! Not the thumbscrews!

I'm sorry. If I gave you the impression that we'd finished with ratchets under "full ratchet anti-dilution," I misled you.

What I'm talking about now are performance-linked ratchets. These little gadgets used to be all the rage. They've now been replaced in popularity by milestone deals, but you still occasionally see them, and they have a big impact on valuation, so I need to say a word or two about them here.

94

Imagine your prospective Vulture looking even more tatty and woebegone than usual, as if he hasn't fed on a corpse for days. He looks like that because you've just told him that based on your projections, your company's going to be worth $100 million by Year 5. You've also told him in no uncertain terms that the $4 million post-money valuation he's proposing is outrageous, because it will give him a 25x return. He's said to you that he aims for 10x, you add, so a valuation of $10 million is fair. Anyway, you've got another investor who's prepared to pay $8 million, so he needs to sharpen his pencil if he wants to do the deal.

He believes that you really do have another investor waiting in the wings. And he really does want to do the deal. He's quite inexperienced, you might judge from his behavior. So he proposes a performance-linked deal, also known as a ratchet.

"OK, then," the Vulture says. "I'll invest $1 million for 20%, which gives you a post-money of $5 million. If you achieve the Year 5 exit of $100 million, you can earn back 10 percentage points of the equity, which will get you back to the $10 million valuation that you want. But we'll have a sliding scale so that if you fall a long way short of the target, my equity will go up to 30%. Fair enough?"

A FINE PERFORMANCE

"Well, I really appreciate your telling me. Thank you for being so straightforward."

"You'd have seen it in the management accounts we have to warrant anyway."

In spite of his disappointment at the news, the Vulture chuckled at the dry tone. He could picture the CFO's wry smile at the other end of the phone. He really liked him – and the rest of the team – and wanted to get the deal over the finishing line.

The CFO continued, "But we do believe in being up front with people. That's how we like to do business."

"It does give me a problem, you know. The main risk I perceived was whether the new product would take off or not. If it's not happening, well, the projected profit that got us to the valuation you wanted won't happen either."

"You never know," said the CFO, injecting some optimism into his normally flat voice. "The prospects are all still there. It is just taking longer to close them than we hoped. It's not surprising really. After all, the new product is a much larger and more strategic sale than we're used to. It is not surprising that it takes longer." He paused. " Look, would you consider a performance-linked deal?"

The Vulture drew in his breath. "I really don't like ratchet deals, you know. Too complicated. And they create a conflict of interest. And I don't like changing the deal after we've given out a term sheet. I wouldn't want you to think that I was taking advantage of the sales blip to walk you backward. It just gets things off to the wrong start."

"Yeah, but I'm the one suggesting it, not you. Look, we want to work with you on this. You said at the beginning that we had pushed you pretty hard on valuation, and that to justify the price we'd have to perform up to budget. We'd be more upset if you walked away, frankly, than if you came back with a performance-related tweak. It's not like we desperately need the money. We can choose whether to take it or not."

"OK. If that's what you really want I'll see what I can do. I'll put a cold towel on my head and have a chat with the other guys here."

The Vulture came back with a proposal that gave the company the agreed valuation if it made budget, but adjusted it down if profits fell short of the £1 million projection for the year in which the investment was made. If the profits were zero, the investor's equity percentage would rise by 50%, and be adjusted on a straight-line basis anywhere in between. This was accepted by the company.

The company did make a loss in the financial period in question, so the effective valuation fell by one third. Nevertheless, everyone was satisfied.

There is an infinite number of variations on the ratchet mechanism, some driven by tax considerations in different regions, but essentially the objective of the ratchet is to dodge the tricky question of valuation up front. Normally it works against the entrepreneur, because normally companies fall short of their objectives (see Chapter 6). But sometimes, as in the example above, it can be a useful tool to help get a deal done. Nevertheless, it always introduces complications and, because it creates a very clear conflict of interest between different shareholders, it can provoke behavior on either side which is not in the best interests of the business overall.

COMPARING TERM SHEETS

Now you understand why your prospective Vulture sounded a bit hesitant, even sheepish, on the telephone when he rang you at the beginning of this chapter to tell you the good news about the term sheet. But wait, the phone's ringing again. Yippee! It's the other investor you were courting. You're going to get a second term sheet!

The venture capital market is imperfect, almost to the point where it isn't a real market at all. You will be in the minority if you find that your second term sheet is directly comparable with your first. There's a high chance that there will be a big enough difference in the proposed structure for the outcome at different valuations to vary quite considerably. Quite possibly one term sheet will produce a better result in one range, and the other will be better above a different level. One may contain more unpalatable peripheral terms. You could be forgiven for thinking that Vultures deliberately structure their term sheets so that they can't be compared directly with their competitors'.

As I promised earlier, the graph below takes the basic deal used as an example in this chapter – $1 million for 25% – and attempts to tabulate the effect of different structures on the outcome at different exit valuations. The proceeds shown are from the management shareholders' perspective, of course.

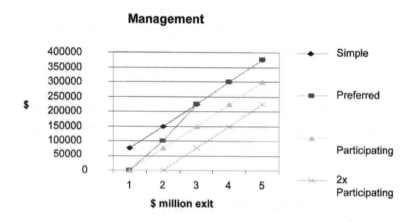

Management

SIMPLE IS BEAUTIFUL

This may all seem appalling complicated. But when you've passed though the second funding round, or the third, you may look back on the relative simplicity of your first round with nostalgia. When several liquidation preferences have been layered on each other, it can become impossible to work out how much of your business you really own, not least because your effective percentage ownership will vary from exit valuation to exit valuation. Wait for Chapter 11.

If you're a technologist you will know about Moore's Law, one of the most famous axioms of the technology industry. It states that the density of transistors on an inexpensive semiconductor will double every two years (initially, when the cofounder of Intel made his observation in an *Electronic Times* article in 1965, he predicted this doubling every year, but in 1975 he revised his view to every two years, since when it has proved remarkably accurate). Gordon Moore did not set out to formulate a law; it was only christened Moore's Law later on, around 1970, by Caltech Professor and VSLI Logic founder Carver Mead. It is often misrepresented as predicting a doubling of transistor density every 18 months, but then most people can't remember the Ten Commandments or the Seven Deadly Sins either.

Acland's Law, which I am about to formulate, is far less distinguished than Moore's Law, but may have some relevance for technology businesses and others who raise multiple rounds of venture capital. Here it is. It states that the difficulty and complexity of negotiating and structuring each venture investment round can be defined as x to the power of y, where x is the complexity of the first round, and y is the number of the current round.

When we come on to Chapter 11 we will cover in more detail the difficulties and complexities that can accumulate when mistakes are made in earlier rounds. For the time being, it's enough to say that one of the main corollaries of Acland's Law is that you should keep your first round as simple as possible, because in the second round the difficulty and complexity of that first round will be squared, in the third round cubed, and so on.

An essential ingredient is keeping the first-round valuation at a sensible level. Yes, that's right, a sensible level, and not pushing it as high as it will go. Ultimately, you are more likely to make more money, and to have more success, if your early-stage investors make money too. You want your second round to take place at a higher price than the first, and your second-round investors to make money too; not as high a multiple of cost as your first investors, but a return that fairly rewards the risk they have taken.

If you try to push your first-round valuation too high, you're almost certain to end up with a more complicated deal structure. The investor's upside will be reduced; therefore he will try harder to limit his downside. So there's a higher chance that anti-dilution or performance-linked instruments will kick in at some point, hitting you with all the force of a mule's hind legs. Also, the chances are that the investor who's willing to chase a deal at a higher price in a more complex structure is less experienced and less successful than the investor who offers a simple and realistic deal. So you run the risk of ending up with a worse investor, in a worse structure, who is more likely to behave unwisely in difficult circumstances. And you will have deserved what you get, because you will have made a bad decision, chasing the headline valuation at all costs, implying that you are a second-rate CEO.

CHAPTER FIVE

Your Deal Breakers

Where do you draw your line in the sand?

In Chapter 3 I mentioned the importance of never getting into a position where you *have* to consummate a particular deal. Always having an alternative is a theme I hope is beginning to echo as often and as loudly in this book as a *leitmotif* in a Wagnerian opera.

Never get into a position where you have to complete a deal at all, let alone where you have to accept investment from a particular investor. If you have no alternative, then you can have no such thing as a deal breaker. Nevertheless, there are some things which *should* be deal breakers. You may feel that the valuation offered, or one of the valuation-impacting structural issues discussed in the previous chapter, makes a deal unattractive to a point where you do not wish to pursue it. That should be pretty clear up front once you have deciphered the term sheet.

This chapter aims to deal with the other terms which arrived in those term sheets but which may only really come into focus in the negotiation over the substantive legal documentation.

LEGAL PRINCIPLES

When I started in the venture capital business in the 1980s the legal documentation in deals was much less standardized and more open to negotiation than it is now. Indeed, the National Venture Capital Association in the US and the British Venture Capital Association now both publish standard Series A investment documentation which is suitable for many circumstances.

I can recommend the latter in particular; I was a member of the committee that was involved in drafting it. Each of them also publishes a comprehensive guide to term sheets, which I equally recommend.

So in theory at least, it should be possible to complete the legal documentation in a venture capital deal with a minimum of fuss and negotiation. Somehow in practice it never seems to work quite like that. I am not a lawyer and this book is not meant to be a legal guide, which I would anyway not be qualified to write. Here I will just take the time to cover in layperson's terms the thinking behind the key areas in an investment agreement.

Vital parts of the documentation establish the structure and share rights which have a direct impact on your deal valuation. The principles of these were covered in the previous chapter. Otherwise, there are three main categories in the legal documents. Here they are, in my view in increasing order of importance but probably in opposite order of length:

1. The sections which define and validate what the investor is investing in (Representations and Warranties).
2. The sections which define how the company is to be run after the investment (Controls and Veto rights).
3. The sections that define what happens if things go wrong and the entrepreneur or other members of the management team leave before the exit (Good Leaver/Bad Leaver conditions).

Note that the word "sections" is plural above. That is because parts of each category are scattered in various places through different documents. In North America there are the Stock Purchase Agreement, Investor Rights Agreement, Voting Agreement, Right of First Refusal and Co-Sale Agreement, and Certificate of Incorporation. In the UK the content of the documentation is broadly the same, but the structure is slightly different, with a Shareholders' Agreement (or Subscription Agreement), Articles of Association, Disclosure Letters, Service Contracts, and so on. I won't even attempt to describe how the documentation and legal structure work in France under Napoleonic principles. I don't really think the lawyers deliberately make it more complicated than necessary in order to justify their existence (and their fees), but sometimes it does seem a bit like that.

REPRESENTATIONS AND WARRANTIES

To provide the investor with as much certainty as possible about the entity in which they are investing, the company itself and its executive directors warrant that a whole series of things about the company are true. When I first started in the business, negotiation about the wording of the warranties could go on all night, but nowadays this is a pretty standard list and it shouldn't really be necessary to argue much about the detailed wording.

This makes a lot of sense, because I'm not aware of one single occasion when legal action has been brought over the warranties in a venture capital agreement. The only circumstances in which a claim is likely to be made under the warranties is in the event of fraud. Note that this is different to the warranties in an acquisition agreement, where claims do sometimes happen (see Chapter 12).

One of the reasons venture capital warranty claims hardly ever take place is that in practice it is unlikely to be in an investor's interest to sue the company in which he is now a shareholder, or members of the management team that he has backed. In the circumstances in which a Vulture is likely to be most inclined to sue – when things have gone badly wrong – he is least likely to gain any practical benefit because there will be little money around. In order to enforce his warranties he will first of all have to prove that he has suffered a loss as a result of a breach of those warranties. Given the number of things that can go wrong in a young business, pinning the blame in court to a warranty breach is not likely to be easy. And if he does manage to enforce his warranties against the company and require it to make good his loss, he may well be destroying any residual value in his investment. If he goes against the management team – well, you know how you would feel about that. For sure the Vulture will have forfeited any remaining goodwill and destroyed any sense of obligation that you might once have felt toward him. So there is little practical point in trying to claim under the warranties. It is just possible that a Vulture might feel so betrayed, deceived, and angry at whatever has happened that he decides to have a go, but then you probably deserve whatever you get. Anyway, as I said earlier, I have never seen it happen, and I have never met anyone who has.

So what is the point of the warranties? Why not just do away with them?

The real purpose of the warranties is to act as a checklist to make sure that the investor has asked about everything, and that the management team has provided all the information that the investor could possibly want. This is done via the mechanism of the Disclosure Schedule, or Disclosure Letter, which lists all the exceptions to the warranties. The idea is that there can be no later recriminations based on a piece of information not being revealed. In this sense the warranties protect you, the entrepreneur, as well as the investor, although it may not feel quite like that when you are the one on the hook.

That hook is less barbed than it used to be, however. Warranty limits (which usually apply in all circumstances except fraud) for management team members used normally to be set at the total amount of the investment being made. Now they are generally set lower, perhaps at one or two years' salary. The dreadful phrase that investors always use when talking about warranty limits is that they should be high enough to "focus the mind," although they sometimes also say, more sympathetically, "We don't want you to lose too much sleep over them." And "joint and several" warranties, where if one warrantor defaults on a warranty claim his share has to be made up by the others (which always seemed to me grossly unfair), have become less common than "several" warranties where each individual is only responsible for his own share.

None of that means that you should not take the warranties seriously, of course. You should approach them with great care and make sure that everything that should have been disclosed has been disclosed. But the only time when the warranties might really break a deal is when the disclosure process throws up an alarming piece of information that puts the investor off proceeding. This part of the legal agreement should never throw up a deal breaker which might cause the entrepreneur to withdraw, unless he really does have something to hide.

CONTROLS AND VETO RIGHTS

Often, especially in the first round of a venture investment, the investors will be buying a minority stake. Thus, theoretically, they are vulnerable to the majority shareholders – normally the management team – decreasing the value of their investment by taking bad decisions, or even exploiting them by stripping value out of the business.

For example, the management team might decide to pay themselves very large salaries, or magnificent bonuses, or (subject to the constraints of company law) a large dividend. Perhaps in these ways they could pay out to themselves most of the money invested. Or it might be possible to sell off the company's main assets, perhaps into an associated vehicle in which the investors had no stake. Some of these essentially fraudulent tricks might be forbidden by legislation, but there are plenty of loopholes that can be exploited.

So it is normal, and reasonable, for the investors to receive protective rights over and above those that might normally attach to their shareholding. These will include the right to receive timely information about the progress of the business (and the right to appoint accountants to get that information if it is not forthcoming), and the ability to veto key decisions which deviate from the company's business plan. That business plan itself will have to be approved annually for the year ahead by the investors.

The investors' rights are virtually all negative until and unless they own a majority of the equity. So although the investors will normally be able to block senior management salary increases or dividend payments, or a sale of the business, they cannot make these things happen. Through the medium of the legal agreements they cannot force the management team to reduce their salaries, nor, generally, can they force a sale of the business.

FIRST REFUSAL AND CO-SALE

In this context, an area which can be contentious is "first refusal and co-sale" (or "drag- and tag-along" in UK parlance). The British names may sound like rules more suitable to a game of football than to the conduct of a business, but essentially they cover what happens if a shareholder wants to sell some or all of his stake to a third party. "Drag-along" rights mean that if shareholders owning, say, 75% of the equity want to sell to a third party, they can require the remaining 25% to sell. Under company law in most jurisdictions, if 90% or 95% of a public company's shares have been acquired by a single party, the balance of 5% or 10% can be compulsorily acquired at the same price. Drag-along rights are the private company equivalent and are normally set with the capitalization table in mind according to which shareholder or group of shareholders should reasonably be able to resist a sale. Sometimes the investor will insist on an absolute veto over the sale of the company.

"Co-sale" or "tag-along" gives shareholders the right to sell some of their shares proportionately alongside other shareholders. So if, say, you are approached by someone wanting to buy 20% of your company, you will not be able just to sell them as many of your shares as you want. You would first have to offer the opportunity to all the other shareholders, so that everyone could sell 20% of their stake if they wanted.

Share transfers are anyway normally subject to a right of first refusal – "pre-emption" in the UK – meaning that if one shareholder wants to sell some or all of his shares, and he has a willing buyer at a particular price, existing shareholders or the company have the right of first refusal to buy those shares at that same price. Only when they have said "no thanks" can the outsider complete the transaction. If all the other existing shareholders wanted to buy the shares, they would normally be allocated pro rata to their shareholdings.

BOARD COMPOSITION

One area on which you need to keep a careful eye is the composition of the board of directors. For of course, it is the board of directors to which the CEO reports. The CEO may run the company day to day, but is subject to the board's scrutiny. The board will take the major decisions, including for example whether to fire the CEO. In the absence of other rules, the shareholders can pass a resolution changing the composition of the board. This is a cumbersome process, requiring notice periods to comply with company law, but so long as you hold a majority of the equity you should be safe... except that certain provisions in both your new Voting Agreement and Certificate of Incorporation (or Shareholders' Agreement and

Articles of Association) may overrule company constitutional norms.

Your investors will certainly expect the right to approve new appointments to the board. They will also expect the right to appoint a director themselves. Sometimes this right is untrammeled; sometimes they have to seek your consent to the individual's identity. Sometimes "such consent is not to be unreasonably withheld." But sometimes, too, they seek the right to appoint more than one director. If you have more than one investor, each of them may have the right to appoint a director. Often the number of directors is subject to a maximum – say seven – and this number is entrenched in the Certificate of Incorporation or Articles of Association. In normal company law it requires a Special Resolution, needing the support of 75% of shareholder votes, to change these constitutional documents. But after Round 1 the consent of investors is likely to be required to change them. So if, say, the investor group has the right to appoint four directors out of a maximum of seven specified in the corporate constitution, they could control your company even without holding a majority stake.

If the investors hold a minority stake after their first-round investment, it is in my view utterly unreasonable for them to seek control of the company through the composition of the board. But if, a round or two later, their shareholding has crept over 50%, then investor board control is harder to argue against, and it may be the management team that will be looking for minority protections through the legal agreements.

If the entrepreneur feels uncomfortable about giving investors standard minority protection rights, frankly you should not be raising money. If you want to retain total control over your company, don't sell any shares in it. But do be aware that at some point in the future the investors may assert one of their veto rights and prevent you from doing what you want. Or you might have to give them an incentive to achieve your goal.

VETO RIGHTS AND WRONGS

"We've been at it now for over 10 years. We want to get on with our lives and do other things. We really do want to sell the business."

The founders looked sorrowfully at their recalcitrant Vulture.

"Sure. I understand that. The trouble is, if we sell now I'm not going to make any money. I want to see us build the company for another couple of years. Then the new products will have worked their way through the system. With the projected top-line growth, profits should have doubled and then I could make a vaguely respectable return."

"At least you won't have lost money. Doesn't the share-holding structure mean that you get all your money back first? You may not make a profit until the price we sell for is higher than the price you came in at, but at least you don't lose money…"

A pregnant pause followed.

"What, you mean like on the other deals I do? Actually, I don't do too badly. And I don't mind losing my money if things go wrong. But when, like here, we've built a good business… I just have to make a profit. I know that I invested at what now looks like a high price, but it was 1999 after all. And the internet side of the business never took off like you projected. But we've built the core software business well – if we make the £7.5 million budget it'll mean fivefold growth in five years. That's not bad in a pretty small market. And it's not like I haven't made a contribution – after all, I brought in the chairman, and I helped find the CEO. Just recently I brought you the CFO when he came out of that other business of ours. You wouldn't have got this far with-out me. So I'm sorry, you need to keep going for another couple of years."

"And what if we won't do that?"

"Well, putting it bluntly, you can't sell the business without my consent. I've got an absolute veto in the Shareholders' Agreement. It is in there for a reason – in case this sort of thing happened. I'm sorry, but there it is. My main obligation is to my fund investors and I'd be failing in my duty to them if I did anything different. I'm not going to change my mind unless I can see my way to doubling my money. If you want to get me there by adjusting the split in the proceeds, then that is your affair."

"You mean that you're asking us to give you some of our money?"

"No, I'm asking you to let the team build the business for another couple of years before we sell. They are up for it, after all. But if you want to make me an offer, that is up to you."

The good offices of the chairman were enlisted to help to negotiate a position where the sale took place and the proceeds were allocated halfway between what the shareholdings implied and what the Vulture wanted.

If you are seriously concerned that the Angel or the Vulture you have chosen might unreasonably block or delay sensible or necessary decisions, then you are taking money from the wrong source and you should think again. Other than an unreasonable attempt by the investor to obtain control by the back door, there should be no real reason for this section of the legal documentation to generate deal breakers.

Do take the time, however, to talk through with your investor how the veto rights will be exercised in practice. Will your personal Mephistopheles be empowered to give consents (clearly the ideal position), or will he have to refer decisions back to the rest of his investment committee, thereby introducing an element of uncertainty and delay?

VESTING, GOOD LEAVERS, BAD LEAVERS, AND OTHER EMPLOYMENT-RELATED PROVISIONS

These are the parts of the legal agreements that often matter most. This is partly because, in my experience, it is the area of the agreement that most often is used, and used in circumstances when there is a conflict between investors and entrepreneur; and partly because it is the area that is least standard and most open to negotiation.

The stock vesting rules, sometimes known as "good leaver/bad leaver" provisions, are designed to deal with what happens to the management team's shareholdings in the event that one of them ceases to be employed by the company. While these rules might be applied in circumstances where one of the team gets bored and decides to leave of their own volition, normally they are invoked in circumstances where the business has not done well and the investors want to see management changes take place. These provisions are especially important if the investor group owns a majority of the equity, because then they can use their majority ownership to force a change in management. But they can also matter when the investors have a minority stake.

As I just said, they often become relevant if the company is doing badly. That means it is probably running out of cash. In such circumstances the investors often have effective control, because without more of their money the company will go bust.

The investor's argument about good leaver/bad leaver provisions will go as follows: "I am backing you, my dear chap. If you leave during the life of the business plan, say in the first five years, the value of my investment will be damaged. And you will have let the side down. So there should be a penalty. Anyway, we'll need some of your shares to incentivize the guy we have to hire to replace you – replacing the irreplaceable, of course."

The entrepreneur is obviously sharp enough to see through the saccharine smile that accompanies that last comment.

"And what if you fire me?" he asks.

"Fire you? Why would we do that? You are the guy we are backing! Anyway, how can we fire you? We do not control the board. And you have a majority, so we cannot appoint more directors without your approval."

In response, the entrepreneur may say that he cannot see why he should give up any of his shares if he leaves either willingly or unwillingly. "After all, they are mine. I bought them in the first place. I have earned them over and over again since. If you kick me out after five years' hard work, why should you be able to get your sticky fingers on my shares? What if you dismiss me unfairly?" I am sure you can imagine the outrage and the indignation creeping into your tone, and the rising volume of the argument.

Ultimately, however, you will have to accept some provisions of this sort as part of the price of raising money. Typically a series of rules will be devised to cater for leaving in different circumstances and after different periods of time. At one end of the scale might be dismissal for gross misconduct, in which case all the leaver's shares have to be sold at a nominal price. At the other end, perhaps, if the leaver can prove unfair dismissal he may be entitled to keep all his shares. Or, macabre though it may be, if you die or are incapacitated you are normally treated as a good leaver and allowed to keep all your shares or sell them at "fair value." In between there may be a sliding scale, allowing you to keep more of your shares if more time has passed, or requiring you to sell some or all of them at the higher of fair value, or the price you paid, or nominal value. The permutations are endless and what can be agreed will vary according to the specific circumstances of your company, as well as from investor to investor. Custom and practice also vary geographically.

The good leaver/bad leaver provisions do not operate only between entrepreneur and investor. They are also of importance between members of the shareholding management team. It may happen that one member of the team does not perform well, or cannot grow with the company, and the decision has to be taken to ask him to go. I have known circumstances where the management team have bitterly regretted negotiating lenient good leaver/bad leaver provisions because one of their number has left under a cloud, kept his equity, and become wealthy as a result of everyone else's efforts. I have also known circumstances where leavers have been allowed to keep some or all of their shares, creating a wide diaspora of small shareholders and as a result causing administrative complexities much regretted by the remaining management.

An added complication is that different aspects of what happens tend to be covered in different documents. The bulk of the provisions about compulsory transfers of shares will be contained in the Articles of Association which govern share rights. In the Shareholders' Agreement there is likely to be a section covering your non-compete obligations if your employment ends. The same clauses may reappear with the rest of your employment terms in your Employment Contract (the non-compete obligations feature in the Shareholders' Agreement as well as the Employment Contract because they are viewed as more enforceable if they are included in the former and are thus linked directly to the investment of a substantial sum in your business). The rules of the share option scheme will have a bearing on whether options can be exercised on leaving employment, and if so how many. And overarching all the corporate documentation will be the general legislation of the jurisdiction in which you are employed.

More often than not, the good leaver/bad leaver or vesting clauses and associated documents are the last parts of the legal documentation to be agreed. It is less likely that you will live to regret where the negotiation ends up in the other two areas. But you may well regret whatever you sign up to in the leaver provisions, so treat them as very real. It is certainly possible that this section of the legal documentation could throw up a deal breaker.

THE REAL POINT OF THE LEGAL PROCESS

Most experienced venture investors view much of the legal process as a tiresome bore. They may delegate a lot of it to their lawyers, or to junior associates. Nevertheless, do not forget that they will be lurking in the background and that contentious points will be referred to them. They may be pulling their lawyers' strings behind the Punch and Judy curtain.

And they will be studying your behavior during the legal process too. They may even be using the process to test you. How does he react to an unreasonable position? Does he roll over when he should not; is he too much of a pushover? Does he have an eye for detail; does he have too much of an eye for detail? Is he unable to delegate? Does he focus on the issues that really matter? Does he listen to advice? The way you handle yourself during the legal process could become a deal breaker – for the investor.

From your point of view, the legal process should be exactly the same: a valuable way to begin the process of getting to know your Angel, Dragon, or Vulture. If he does not handle himself well during the process and breathes fire all over you, it will be a sign of things to come. If he is slow, obdurate, hectoring, unreasonable, or runs to his colleagues – his investment committee – for approval of every clause, that is a good guide to how he will behave when he is a shareholder and a member of your board. If you really do not like what you see, walk away before it's too late.

And most important of all, if he tries to walk you backward, walk away. If you find your investors trying to change the terms of your deal for no good reason other than a desire to improve their position, you should think very hard before signing up with them, even if they eventually back down. Behaving in this way is duplicitous, in the sense that it is going back on something they have agreed to do, and it is stupid. It is stupid because it will get the all-important relationship between entrepreneur and investor off to a bad start. It is that relationship as much as anything else that will determine the success of the investment and how much money the investors make. If your investors take unreasonable advantage of you at the beginning, you will mark it down and make a resolution to wreak revenge at a later date. In all probability the investors will end up making less money as a result.

But you don't want to get into a position where you have to swallow an unreasonable position, or accept unpalatable behavior from your venture capital beast, and hope to get your own back later. If you have your Plan B, you won't have to.

INTELLIGENCE THAT IS NOT ARTIFICIAL

The conference room in the bowels of the lawyer's office was windowless. It had been a mistake to strip the sandwiches of their clingfilm. They stale-scented the air as their edges curled slowly upward under the heat of the overhead lights. The glare bounced off the highly polished table. The man who sat drumming his fingers impatiently on its surface felt a headache coming on.

A younger man marched aimlessly up and down. He stopped. "Why is he so late? Bloody scientists. They have no sense of time. We've got so much signing to do. We'll be here all night." He gesticulated at the neatly squared piles of paper on the table, the shareholders' agreement, the articles of association, the board minutes, the disclosure bundles. His incipient anger betrayed that this was only his second deal.

The seated man, the syndicate leader, more senior and more relaxed, drawled at the third person, perched on the

---

edge of a side table, "Give him another call, would you? After all, you are his corporate finance adviser."

The keypad beeped the now familiar tune. In the silent anticipation that filled the room along with the sandwich smell, they could all hear the ring at the other end of the line... and then the voicemail message. Then they jumped as another phone on the side table jangled loudly.

The younger venture capitalist stopped pacing. The corporate finance adviser quickly picked up the receiver. He listened for a moment. His face turned pale. He slammed the phone back down.

"My God. He has just signed another deal. He decided to sell the company instead. No, I didn't know anything about it – I hadn't the faintest clue. After all, I'm only on a success fee."

Not for nothing was the proprietor one of the leading proponents of artificial intelligence software in Europe.

CHAPTER SIX

Managing Your New Partner

...not having a new managing partner

If you have done your due diligence well, you will not only have made sure that you have chosen the right investment partner; you should also have gained some useful hints about what to expect and how to get the best out of your new relationship.

All venture capital firms like to talk about their "added value" or "value add," the benefits they can bring to your company in addition to their money. Their added value is important to them for a number of reasons. First of all, they are used to talking to their customers about it. Remember from Chapter 2 that these fortunate customers are not the companies in which they invest, or you and the team they have backed, but their own fund investors, their beloved LPs. Vultures like talking to their LPs about added value in the same way that entrepreneurs like talking to their customers about their product features. It sounds impressive and is considerably easier than discussing the more quantifiable and less forgiving subjects of returns, pricing, and cost benefits.

Although different firms emphasize different areas in which they can add value, the broad themes are pretty similar. Most will claim generic expertise in building businesses. "The same issues crop up again and again," they say. "I've been doing this for ten years and frankly there isn't much that I haven't seen before. But if there is, well, we've got strength in depth in this firm, and one of my partners will have seen it before in the unlikely event that I haven't."

Most will talk about being able to help with key financial events. "When it comes to the next funding round, you'll find we're pretty well plugged in. And for the exit we know all the good M&A brokers, and the investment bankers if we – you – decide to go the IPO route."

Some mention their range of contacts. "As a firm, we've got a pretty good Rolodex. We can open a lot of doors for you at a senior level." That always makes me want to ask why they haven't yet moved into the computer age and set up a proper contact database, but the term Rolodex seems to have sunk deep into the jargon. "And when you need to hire a chief marketing officer you'll find we're in touch with the right people."

"All our companies need to grow internationally, of course. We'll definitely be able to help develop your strategy. China? Yes, of course. And the other BRICs? Naturally."

"We really know your sector well. After all, it's the area we specialize in."

A lot of this can be true. To an extent. Most established venture firms will indeed have seen a lot before. They will have worked with any number of professional advisers of different sorts. They will have some useful contacts, maybe even in the overseas territories into which you want to grow. And they may even know some things about your sector that you don't know yet.

However, you do need to be realistic. Your circumstances, your needs, will be subtly different from most of the other companies your investor has backed. One size does not fit all in the venture capital business. And you need to be careful that you are not being squeezed into an ill-fitting shirt, in case you find yourself angrily bursting out of it later on like some incredible hulk.

From time to time I have seen venture firms come up with useful contacts. Sometimes they really do happen to know that elusive chief marketing officer who has experience in your sector, lives in the right place, and is looking for a job just when you are recruiting. But a lot has to come together at once. So more often you will find yourself hiring an executive search company as usual.

Sometimes the investor may be able to provide you with a senior contact in an enterprise that you want to make a customer, or a partner. Sometimes going to see that senior individual can help to eliminate an obstacle lower down the organization; but sometimes it can solidify the blockage in the pipe, because the mid-ranking decision maker resents the embarrassing telephone call from the person four rungs further up. High-level contacts can sometimes be counterproductive, and they are never a substitute for good sales skills and a compelling commercial case.

So if you expect your Vulture to carry a magic wand in his briefcase, you will be disappointed. It is full of the usual stuff: documents, old magazines, used itineraries, and the latest iPhone. The number of investors who can really change the fortunes of your company are few and far between, and whether even these venture capital superstars – these lammergeiers of the venture world – make a major difference or not may depend to an extent on luck.

Be realistic. You should be looking for support, good sense, and calm advice from your Vulture. The contacts you are most likely to get from him will be professionals on the periphery of the Vulture's world, people who can help with your share option scheme, or your patent application, or, yes, that M&A transaction. These may well be useful. But do not be surprised if you get one recommendation from one investor, and another from another. Professional firms, and even individuals, sometimes do a good job, and sometimes not. Sometimes they click and sometimes they slip.

A good analogy is a soccer game. The entrepreneur is on the field with the executive team alongside. The investors and the non-executive directors are the fans in the bleachers or the stands. They've watched lots of games. They'll be good at shouting advice. A few of them may have played something in their time, but not many of them will have performed in your sport at your level. Those who have been performers in the past may well be used to an earlier era of the game. It has probably changed a lot since their day. In any event, you don't really want them to invade the pitch and try to join in.

Nor is it likely to impress the fans much if you shout up at them continuously for help. If you make it too obvious that there are serious deficiencies in your game, you may find that their cheers turn to boos and they start shouting for changes to the team before the next trade deadline, or before the transfer window closes.

There is an important balance to get right here. You need to be open to the help offered by your investor. Welcome it and follow up assiduously any contacts he provides, so that if they do not deliver what is hoped for at least it isn't your fault. By all means ask for advice and assistance, but do so in a way that does not display weaknesses that you, as a CEO, should not have. It is all about effective communication.

YOUR *KEIRETSU*

Before you can communicate effectively you must understand the person with whom you are trying to connect. The point of the careful reference checking you did on your investor before deciding to take his money was to help you to understand him before you had the chance to get to know him yourself.

One of the valuable by-products of your due diligence exercise should be the contacts with other chief executives. Remember the people you talked to? Make a point of maintaining those contacts. Many good venture capital firms will bring their portfolio companies together once a year, or at least will bring together those businesses which are relevant to each other. Some of them talk about building a *keiretsu*, after the Japanese term for a loose-knit alliance of corporations. Build your own *keiretsu*, and develop a group of CEOs with whom you exchange news and views on a regular basis.

Whenever my firm brought portfolio companies together, the chief executives concerned acknowledged it as one of our most effective ways of adding value. Some of this was doubtless because of the benefit of talking to each other directly about general issues without the filter or intermediation of an investor. But my ears also used to burn; I am sure it was equally useful for CEOs to talk to each other about me: "Did he help you with that?" "Was so-and-so any good when he introduced you?" "Why does he have a bee in his bonnet about that?" and so on.

So build your own *keiretsu* and use it as a short cut to learning more about your investor, and to explaining any behavior which may seem strange.

TWO-WAY COMMUNICATION

Another essential for effective communication with your investor is clear, open dialogue. One of the main forums for this is the board meeting, but this is so important (and has so many opportunities to go seriously wrong) that I have devoted the whole of the next chapter to it.

Make a point of establishing regular lines of communication with your investor outside the board meeting as well. Encourage your investor to feel involved by ringing him to share significant news, or to ask specific advice.

Of course, the news you want to share is the good news. "You remember the lead we were discussing at the last board meeting? Well, we've got the purchase order now. Yes, actually it's a little bit bigger than we'd hoped." That conversation feels really good – at both ends of the phone.

However, sharing only the good news is like shouting out the score in tennis only when you're winning; after a while it becomes very irritating. Venture capitalists are cynical creatures.

I have often heard or taken part in the following conversation in my office:

"Have you heard from Greg/Charlotte/Rohan recently?"

"No, he hasn't been in touch for a week or so."

"I suppose that means things aren't going as well as he hoped."

"Ha!" (bitter laugh) "Yes, probably. Maybe I'd better give him a ring."

So from time to time, ring up your Vulture and say that the order has slipped, or gone away. Taking the trouble to share bad news builds trust and creates the opportunity to end the conversation on a positive note: "They decided to stick with the competition on this occasion... but the integrator we were working with was so impressed with our pitch that they now want to take us in to another of their customers..."

If the Vulture had made the call, ending the conversation like this would sound defensive. If you initiate the call, it's clear that you're not being defensive.

In Chapter 2 I talked about the pressures on venture firms, and the individuals who make them up. From time to time, as well as telling your investor about your progress, ask him how things are going in his business. Let him know that you keep up with what he is doing or offer help.

"I saw from your website that you've just made a new investment. That looked interesting."

"Of course, you know that I would be delighted to act as a reference if companies you are looking at investing in want to do due diligence with your existing portfolio. I hope that goes without saying."

"When is your annual investor meeting? If you want any portfolio companies to come and present at it I'd be very keen to do so."

The way your Vulture reacts to these offers of help is a good test of the way you are viewed. If you are used as a reference, it is a sign that your investor believes you have a good relationship and trusts you to say the right things. If you are invited to the annual investor meeting, it means that yours is viewed as one of the companies in the portfolio with high potential, and that your presentational skills are highly rated.

Try to keep tabs on how your own Vulture is doing in his firm. But also make sure that you develop a relationship with his colleagues, his peers, and, even more importantly, if he is not a senior partner, with his superiors. If you want, or need, to raise another round of funding, support from your existing investor will be a collective decision of the firm, not just your own Vulture's call. So if you go to a meeting in his office, try to engineer an opportunity to say "hi" to some of the others there too. Maybe there's an excuse to borrow a desk in the open-plan office for a while.

Anyway, if the other people in the firm are smart, they will want to get to know you better. Whenever I saw CEOs in my office from portfolio companies that were the responsibility of other people in my team, I would make a point of going to chat to them. It wasn't that I didn't trust my colleagues' judgment (heaven forbid!). There's just no substitute for a bit of direct eye contact of your own.

WHY YOU WANT A CHAIRMAN

If you're now suffering a sense of *déjà vu*, it's because I've touched on this before. In Chapter 3 we talked about how a chairman can help with the fundraising process. I warned then that I would make your need for a chairman one of my *leit-motifs*; just like the need for a fall-back plan at all times.

Some chief executives like to combine their role with being chairman as well. In the US this is perhaps more frequent than in the UK and Europe. This is one definite example of Europe being right and the US being wrong.

Some chief executives seem to think that having a chairman can threaten their position or dilute their authority. But in fact a good, independent chairman is the best ally a chief executive can have.

First of all, however open your relationship with your Vulture, there are some things you may not want to say directly to him.

"Fred, I thought your comments in the last board meeting were really unhelpful. Fred, I was really disappointed that you did not follow up on the actions you promised. Fred, you really do need to sort out the bonus scheme, because I and my team are beginning to get demotivated."

None of these statements is calculated to foster a friendly relationship with your Vulture. For your chairman, though, it is easy:

"Fred, I think you could have couched your comments at the board in a slightly more constructive way. I could just see Jane beginning to take umbrage. I know you didn't mean to rub her up the wrong way, but she's rightly sensitive to suggestions that she hasn't thought things through. I think that's fair enough, don't you? How would you feel in the same circumstances?"

"Fred, I know Jane would really appreciate it if you could dig out that contact that you promised. It is great to talk about your Rolodex, good to open it, and even better to deliver the name."

"Fred, we really do need to get the bonus scheme agreed and implemented. Jane was saying to me that she's getting worried about the motivation of a couple of members of the team. We really don't want to run the risk of losing our good people."

Secondly, of course, the chairman can act as a conduit for uncomfortable messages from your Vulture.

"Jane, Fred thought that you handled those contract negotiations really badly. He was happy to tell you what he thought face to face, but I said I would chat to you about it. To be honest, I can see his point. We do need to make sure that we do it better next time."

Although in these circumstances the chairman is another link in the pipe, he helps rather than hinders the open flow of communication. He can make sure that things are said that otherwise might be left to fester unhealthily until a later occasion, when they erupt with the virulence of a cholera outbreak. He can use his age and his authority to weight the message appropriately, making it clear that in his view it is wholly or only partly reasonable – or not at all reasonable and to be ignored. His involvement can prevent a confrontation that may damage a relationship. In part this is because the CEO and the Vulture need to feel that they are equals, peers. If they lock horns like rutting stags on an issue and fight for superiority, the equality of the relationship can be damaged. The chairman can help to maintain the necessary balance.

Of course, for the chairman to be effective he must be truly independent of both the entrepreneur and the investor. If the investor feels that the chairman has "gone native" and is just a cipher for the CEO, then he will be worse than useless. Equally, the chairman loses his point and purpose if the entrepreneur thinks that he is just a Vulture in disguise. So the entrepreneur needs to accept that from time to time a good chairman will tell him that he is wrong and that the Vulture is right. Even the best CEO is not infallible; and only the bad ones think they are.

THE ANGEL CHAIRMAN

At the risk of more repetition from Chapter 3, let me say again that I have often found that the best dynamic is having an experienced Angel as chairman. This is because the best Angels straddle the investor/entrepreneur gap and genuinely have a foot on each side of that chasm. An Angel is likely to be senior in age and experience to both the CEO and the Vulture, and able to gain and hold the respect of both. He will typically have had the experience of running a business and so will have empathy with the entrepreneur and lessons to share. He will also sympathize with the investor's concerns, being one himself. Having a stake in the business is likely to hold his attention more fully than a chairman who has simply been hired to do the job.

If your Vulture is relatively young, and still capable of learning, you may also have done the world of venture capital and entrepreneurship a service, for working with a really good Angel may well turn the Vulture into a far better investor.

So, as I suggest in Chapter 2, if you can identify the right Angel to invest in your business in the first round, and to join your team in the role of chairman, you will get off to a good start.

DO YOU SOCIALIZE WITH VULTURES?

The obvious answer to this question is "Well, not normally, not if I can help it." The same answers probably apply to socializing with Dragons and Angels too. Or maybe your mother-in-law is a dragon and your children are little angels.

The way you build your relationship with your new investor depends on many things, of course. Primarily, it depends on you and the way you feel comfortable building your important business relationships. If you build your relationship with your team in a particular way, or with your major customers, and you find that works for you, apply the same formula to building your relationship with your investor. Just don't forget how important that relationship is.

It is definitely worth spending time with your Vulture, Angel, or Dragon in an informal setting away from the office. Long, extravagant lunches are unlikely to impress, nor is an expensive box at a sporting event organized just for his benefit. He will feel that you are not spending his money wisely. But including your Vulture with some customers in an afternoon's corporate entertainment, or in a team-building event, could have all sorts of advantages. If you do, just make sure he is briefed first about who is who and what you want to achieve from him. You might be pleasantly surprised by how much the Vulture can help. And do ask him to the office Christmas party; unless there is really something wrong with your team, the benefits will be well worth any embarrassing moments!

CHAPTER SEVEN

Board Meetings

How not to be bored

Before you had investors you may scarcely have had board meetings. You always have held regular management meetings, of course – or so I hope – with your senior team. These are an essential part of the mechanism which you use to run the business. But you may have held board meetings once in a while as a tiresome formality to approve accounts and other occasional paperwork, with little relevance to the day-to-day running of the business.

After a venture investment you will have to hold regular board meetings. The legal documentation will usually specifically say that each year you must hold twelve board meetings, or ten, or eight, or maybe six. What on earth are they for? Why do you have to bother?

Entrepreneurs who underestimate the importance of the board meeting in their brave new post-investment world do so at their peril. Good board meetings can be valuable and move a company several steps along the way. Bad board meetings can be deadly dull, desperately damaging, and downright destructive.

OH SHIT

Think about your board meetings from the point of view of the new member of the board, your investor. Unless he is very young and this is one of his first deals, he will probably sit on quite a number of other boards. At one point I was on twelve at once, including four public companies. Or was it fourteen?

Some might have seen that as a high point in their career; to me it was a low point and I nearly went berserk. However, that, or even more, is the load to which some Vultures subject themselves. More often, and more sensibly, they will try to limit the number to half a dozen.

However many boards your Vulture sits on, those meetings are likely to afford him his main viewpoint on what is happening in the companies he has backed. In the industry jargon, the first board meeting after an investment completes is known as the "Oh shit" board meeting, because it is there that the process of finding out what you have invested in really begins. All experienced venture investors know that, however meticulous their pre-investment due diligence, they will learn much more about the company they have backed and the market it addresses, and the people in its team, after the deal is done than before.

At partners' meetings throughout the industry, often held on Monday morning – presumably in order to wipe away the benefits of the weekend as fast as possible – the following conversation will be repeated:

"So how are things going at Xcorp, then?"

"Well, actually, I am there for a board meeting on Thursday. And I haven't had the papers yet so I am not totally up to speed. Could we discuss it next week?"

WHOSE MEETING?

I bet you can already see one of the problems inherent in the board meetings of venture-backed businesses. It is your company's board meeting, of course, not the investor's, but the meeting is taking place at the investor's behest, and to some extent for the investor's benefit.

Nevertheless, do not allow it in any circumstances to become the Vulture's meeting. It is your company's board meeting, and so it should remain. When the board members are sitting around that table together, the primary role and legal obligation of each one is as a director of the company, whether he is Angel, Dragon, Vulture, or entrepreneur. Make sure that it stays that way, and that board meetings are for the benefit of your company, not for the benefit of one individual member of the board, whether Vulture or anyone else.

There is plenty that you can do – with a bit of help from your chairman, for managing the board effectively is another vital part of his role – to make sure that these meetings work to everyone's advantage. However, many times the basic rules are forgotten.

A FEW PRE-BOARD DOS AND DON'TS

Don't ask the investor what he would like to see on the agenda and what information he would like in the board pack. It may seem polite, welcoming, and well-intentioned to do so, but if you do, you will have started racing down the track of making it his meeting, not yours. You may also have given the impression that you do not know what information is needed to run your business.

Do consider what you would want to see if you were in the investor director's shoes, and set about providing it.

Do think about what you want to show your investor. By this, I do not mean that you should censor the information you provide. You have a legal and moral obligation to be completely open. It is also the only sensible approach because, if you try to conceal unwelcome information, it will emerge eventually with calamitous consequences. What I mean is that you should think carefully about how you present your information so that the important points stand out.

Do remember that you know a great deal more about your business, especially at the beginning of a relationship, than your investor. Remember also that while running your company is your main activity, your investor has many other things on his plate. Your company is important to him. He wants you to succeed. Your success will help his success. But he has many other worries and concerns, and some of those may matter more to him than your company does. As we established in Chapter 2, you are not his customer, and you may not be his most important product. You have to make it easy for him to get the information he needs.

Don't swamp him with too much indigestible information in order to fill the all gaps in his knowledge at once.

Do make sure that every page in the board pack is as clear and as comprehensible to someone who is learning about the business as it is to an insider.

Do make sure that the board pack exposes how you run your business. You want your investor to know that you have a feel for the key metrics. Show him what you think is important. If you are burning cash and are pre-revenue, the number of months of overhead covered by your cash balance is likely to be a key metric. If your cost of sale has a major impact on profitability, then gross margin may be especially important. If the effectiveness of your marketing spend is the main driver of revenue growth, then marketing metrics should perhaps be at the front of your mind. Each business is different, but do show the investor that you think about yours in a clear and coherent way.

Do make sure that the management accounts are clear, that they include the information you are obliged by the Investor Rights or Shareholders' Agreement to include, and that they compare actual results consistently against the budget that your investor expects. It may be that your investor has more of a financial background than you do, so take particular care to master your business's financial vital statistics such as the budget for the year, the monthly overhead, the burn rate, the revenue needed for breakeven, and so on.

Don't leave all the understanding of the financials to your chief financial officer or finance director. By all means leave him to explain the accounting detail, but make sure you understand all the important aspects yourself. The Vulture will rightly expect this of a rounded CEO.

Don't use endless unexplained TLAs. They may be common usage to you and your team, but either your outside director may not understand them and get the wrong end of some stick as a result, or he will have to spend the board meeting asking what they mean and will become increasingly irritated at exposing what you have made him feel is ignorance. (By the way, in this context TLA stands for Three Letter Acronym, not Tender Love and Affection – and isn't it irritating?)

Don't send the board pack out by email the day before the meeting.

Don't send it out on Friday evening for Monday morning and imply that you expect the investor to read it over the weekend. Many Vultures spend a lot of time traveling. A lot of them rely on their BlackBerries to keep in touch. I know from bitter experience that it is not easy to read a set of management accounts on a BlackBerry, and when I've been forced to try to do so by an inconsiderate CEO, I tend to arrive at a board meeting underbriefed and overheated.

Don't send the board pack out in dribs and drabs. If you do, it will look as if your team are disunited and do not communicate. You will look disorganized and will increase the likelihood that an important document has gone missing and has not been read.

Do find out in what format your Vulture likes to receive the board pack.

Do deliver it to him in his preferred format, whether electronic or hard copy, so that he gets it at least three working days before the meeting. Call, or have someone call, his assistant to make sure that he is not traveling in the days before the meeting, so that your good intentions to get him his papers well in advance are not thwarted.

Do make sure that the board papers make sense of the company's progress on their own. Many a time I have called down curses on a CEO – or a CFO – as I scrabble back through a file to try to relate May's sales report to April's, and to track whether the large order that is now predicted for July has come forward since the previous month (unlikely) or slipped back (more likely!). Then, when I finally work out that slippage has indeed occurred, I am irritated because it is bad news, and doubly irritated because I have had to spend precious time digging up the data. I may even be so irritated that I begin to suspect my friends the CEO and CFO of obfuscation and of deliberately burying unwelcome information.

Do set your board meetings for a time in the month when it will be possible to provide the necessary information in a reliable way. Normally the gating factor is the availability of management accounts. You will not win any points for holding your meeting in the second week of the month instead of the third, or even in the third instead of the fourth. But you will lose plenty of points if the management accounts are sent out on the eve of the meeting after the rest of the board papers have been circulated, or if they are handed out at the meeting itself. Why create unnecessary pressure for yourself?

Do fix a program of meetings for the year ahead. Remember that your Vulture may have half a dozen board meetings to fit in every month, or even more. If you don't fix yours well in advance for a time that suits you, one of his other portfolio companies will take the slot that you want. Often Vultures' board meetings get concentrated in the third week of the month when most companies have their management accounts available; there may be something to be said for holding yours a little later.

Don't change the dates of your meetings from the advance schedule except for a matter of life and death. They will be a nightmare to rearrange because of the pressures on most Vultures' diaries. But more importantly, it gives out the message that you do not value the board meetings and by extension the participants in them. It is far better to suggest at the previous meeting that because everything is going smoothly and there are no strategic issues to discuss, it may not be necessary to hold a board meeting the following month. Or to transmute it into a telephone meeting.

You have probably skimmed through this section incredulously, thinking to yourself "Why is he telling me this, it is blooming obvious?" Yes, it is blooming obvious, but I still struggle to think of a single portfolio company with which I have been involved in the last 25 years that has followed these simple rules with absolute consistency.

Sometimes board meetings collapse into a question-and-answer session between investor and entrepreneur in spite of all these rules being followed, because the investor has not taken the trouble to read and understand the board pack. If that happens more than once, then it falls to your chairman to take the investor director to one side and ask, in the nicest possible way, what the problem is. But far more often, in my experience, board meetings degenerate into Q&A because inadequate information has been badly presented at short notice. If you get it right, you should be set up for a productive and efficient meeting which will deliver your objectives. You should be set up for a meeting which will be *your* board meeting.

YOUR PLACE OR MINE?

I remember squirming with embarrassment when, the morning after my first date with my future wife, I found myself having breakfast with her mother. Yes, we had gone back to her place. But actually it all worked out for the best in the end. Breakfast with my delightful future mother-in-law somehow seemed to cement my relationship with her daughter.

The "your place or mine" question for board meetings is not much different. Often there is some pressure to use your investor's office for board meetings. Or if there is no pressure, the offer of a room for the meeting can be a tempting one. The chances are that your investor's office will be more conveniently located than yours. It will probably have more, bigger, better conference rooms, and maybe stronger coffee.

You may also remember that the sound-proofing in your office is not quite perfect, that the projector screen in the main boardroom can be seen from the door, and that your receptionist's charming telephone manner barely compensates for her ability to make all drinks taste like dishwater. Then there is that brilliant but eccentric member of your software development team who has an uncanny knack of hanging around the water cooler and asking awkward questions just at the moment when important visitors appear. It is perhaps not quite as embarrassing as breakfast with your new girlfriend's mother, but there are still plenty of things that can go wrong.

Suddenly the thought of a board meeting at the investor's place in Sand Hill Road or Mayfair seems rather attractive. Don't be tempted. Get ye behind me, Satan! Remember that it is *your* board meeting, and that the default location should be your place, not theirs. Once you begin holding your meetings at your investor's office, they start to become more his meetings than yours. Instead of your board meetings being about your corporate strategy and tactics, they begin to feel like a visit to the headteacher's study to give a monthly account of yourself, and perhaps to receive a smart caning.

When I was working as a Vulture I hated having portfolio company board meetings in my own office. And this is the other side of the coin. To really understand what was going on in the business I had backed, I liked to go to its office at least once a month and have a good look at what was going on. If the meeting was first thing in the morning, I would try to get there early and see what time staff arrived. If it started in the middle of the afternoon, I liked to wander around after it was over and see how many of the team were still at their desks after hours. If I couldn't do that, I could get clues about how things were going just from being in the office, breathing the air, watching the faces, and looking at whatever scrawl was left on the whiteboards. I used to make a point of getting to know salespeople, developers, secretaries, as many people below board level as possible, in order to get a feel for what the board pack could or would not tell me. Call me sly, nosy, or suspicious if you like, but actually I was just doing my job as a nonexecutive director properly and finding out enough about the company to take good decisions when necessary.

So there is a risk in choosing your own place. But if you are not confident enough to expose your company to the scrutiny of a fellow director and co-shareholder, then there's probably something seriously wrong which needs fixing.

YOUR AGENDA

You have provided all the necessary information for your fellow directors and chosen your venue. What should you actually talk about at the meeting?

If a meeting lasts one minute longer than three hours it has lasted one minute too long. The best board meetings last two hours. Three is just about acceptable, but any longer than that and people lose concentration, their eyelids droop, they lose energy and get bored or irritable, and all the careful preparation you have done goes to waste.

So, with your chairman, make sure that the agenda will not run beyond that time limit, and construct it accordingly. The dynamic of each board will be different, and it will take two or three meetings for a new group of directors to settle down together and for the ideal format to emerge. All board meetings start with the formality of approving the minutes of the last meeting, and then most run through a list of actions attached to the minutes. I am skeptical that this is really the best thing to do – the action list often comprises unimportant items, accumulated in a random order, and the opening energy of the meeting can dissipate on trivia. Personally, I prefer to get straight to the meat of the meeting, and deal with the board papers that have been sent out.

Because you have followed my advice and carefully thought through the content of the board reports, and because you have made sure that they were sent out well in advance, it should not normally be necessary to spend much more than half an hour on them. Nor is it necessary to repeat in a long, verbal preamble what they already contain in writing. A brief introduction should be all that is needed, highlighting the key issues, and perhaps giving an update if significant things have occurred in the short space of time since the papers were prepared.

Then, having disposed of the current issues, there should be time for two, or possibly three, topics about which you want to take a decision in the medium to longer term. These might be to do with future product direction and development, or whether, when, and how to penetrate a new geographical territory. Or you might want to discuss why your marketing strategy is less effective than you might wish, or which corporate alliances you want to seal. Whatever the topics are, they should be the issues which concern you most in the medium term – far enough away for a measured discussion to take place before a decision has to be made, but close enough for some specifics to be discussed. As with the routine board papers, the more advanced context and thinking time you are able to give the outside members of the board, the more fruitful your discussion is likely to be.

In a young venture-backed business the pressures are sometimes such that everything gets concertinaed so that only immediate issues get discussed. The company seems to bounce from crisis to crisis. Do not allow this to happen – think ahead, and get your fellow directors to think ahead too.

You raised venture capital in order to allow your company to make losses and invest, or consume, cash. So one of the key issues for regular consideration at board meetings will be cash flow breakeven and funding strategy. You must not lose the initiative in this critical area, even if, as is likely, you feel your venture capital beast has more experience and expertise on this subject than you. Too many times I have seen CEOs forfeit their authority in that awful moment when they turn to their Vulture with a nervous smile and say, "Well, now we had better talk about the next funding round. Sally, this is your area. What do you think we should do?"

Or even worse, the Vulture turns round toward the end of the meeting, under "Any Other Business," and says with an uncomfortable squawk, "The cash flow projections show us running out of money in eight months' time. Shouldn't we be talking about the options?" Shocked faces all round, and mutterings in the corridor after the meeting between Vulture and chairman about whether the CEO is up to the job.

Instead, you should lead the conversation like this: "As you can all see from the cash flow projections, the probability is that we will be out of cash in eight months' time. That is a couple of months earlier than we originally expected, as we've had a little sales slippage, although we have balanced that by tight overhead control. Anyway, I'd like to start discussing our options now.

"As I see it, there is a possibility that the large sale we were discussing earlier might land in time – that's option one – but I do not want to rely on that. We've looked at what we'd have to do to reduce the overhead to bring it in line with revenue; that is option two and would mean going down to eight people within six months. We'd be able to survive, but obviously it would mean giving up our growth ambitions.

"Option three is that our relationship with A Corporation is developing quite nicely. I can see the possibility that they might offer us some cash up front in return for distribution rights in their home market, and sometimes they take small stakes in businesses which have technology which might be strategic to them. But I don't want to have to force it, even though we could talk to a couple of their competitors to keep them honest. And of course, the conversation might just lead to an offer for the whole shooting match, but in an ideal world it is too early for that.

"So the fourth option is to do another funding round, either internally or bringing in a new investor. Sally, do you have any views about that?"

WHO SHOULD COME TO THE MEETING?

Well, the directors of the company, obviously.

But it isn't quite that simple. The only executive directors of the company after the investment round may be the CEO, the CFO, and your co-founder, the chief technology officer. Or you may be the only executive director. You've been used to those management meetings, with all the members of your team – including the new chief marketing officer, the head of sales, and the VP of product development – there to talk about their functional area. Shouldn't they come to the board meeting? Then the outside directors would be able to hear it from the horse's mouth.

At one point in my Vulture career I did think that having all the members of the management team in the board meeting, and hearing it from the horse's mouth, was a good idea. But I changed my mind. It is important to be able to judge how much of a grip the CEO has on all the functional areas. You can always have a conversation after the board meeting directly with the head of sales or indeed with individual salespeople. In the board meeting the investor wants to observe how much the CEO knows about the sales pipeline, and the CEO should demonstrate his knowledge and the grip he has on the business.

The board may also need to be able to discuss the performance of the members of the team, and to get the CEO's views on them. And on occasion I have seen real damage done by all-inclusive board meetings, as the technically brilliant but financially naïve head of development's eyes glaze over with boredom when the management accounts are discussed and then fill with alarm once it becomes apparent that the Vulture isn't automatically going to lay down a check to cover the hole in the cash flow.

Of course, that isn't to say that key individuals can't be invited to join the meeting. When a discussion about marketing strategy is being held it would indeed be a little odd if the CMO were not asked to present their thoughts. It is helpful to expose other members of the team to the full board, and vice versa, from time to time. But when you do bring members of your team into the meeting, make sure that you've briefed them fully and made the objectives clear.

SOME ENTERTAINMENT

And from time to time, at the end of a board meeting, throw in some entertainment. I don't mean a song-and-dance routine and a bit of air guitar by those heavy metal fans in software development. I mean show the outside directors a demonstration of the latest product features. Or bring in one of the sales team to repeat part of the excellent pitch they did last week. I know in a way that I may be contradicting my earlier comment that the board meeting should be about running the company, not primarily about passing out information. But it is well worth putting on a good show from time to time. You end the meeting on a positive note and remind the Vulture, or the Angel or Dragon, why he invested in your company in the first place. And you help him to do his job of adding value by enabling him to talk more effectively about your product and its USPs (sorry, there I go again, ignoring my own advice – I mean Unique Selling Points).

THE CHAIRMAN AGAIN

At times in this chapter I may have talked as if you are in charge of your board meeting, but of course this isn't the case. Your chairman is. You are the soloist in the concerto, but your chairman is the conductor, bringing out the big themes, moving the music forward neither too slowly nor too fast, and making sure that the members of the orchestra are in time with you and that the whole thing doesn't descend into a dreadful dissonant cacophony.

I know that some soloists conduct the orchestra. Very occasionally it works (try those wonderful recordings of Mozart Piano Concertos with the matchless Murray Perahia both as soloist and conductor of the English Chamber Orchestra). More often it does not, however. It is hard, when you are doing much of the talking, also to manage the meeting.

Of course, for it to work, the conductor needs to have spent plenty of time with the soloist before the concert. He also needs to have rehearsed the orchestra. The chairman's discussion with the CEO about the objectives of the board meeting and how best to handle it, and his calls to the outside board members to see if they have any issues or concerns ahead of the meeting, are an important part of the preparation.

THE WORST MEETINGS OF ALL

I'm sorry, folks, I owe it to all the CEOs who have suffered to say this. The worst board meetings of all are where the majority of directors sitting around the table are Vultures. There have been too many funding rounds and too many investors have insisted on a board seat. Too much money has gone in because things have slipped and the CEO's credibility is damaged. Everyone is nervous and bad tempered. Passing on the blame has become the name of the game. Even a good chairman is pretty helpless to stop the Vultures showing off to each other, laying into the management team, flashing their BlackBerry, iPhone 4, or other latest gadget, scoring points, and worrying about whether the meeting will be finished in time for them to catch that first-class intercontinental flight.

Beware of getting yourself into this position!

CHAPTER EIGHT

Managing Expectations

Setting expectations low makes them easier to beat

Well, I hear you say, that last chapter was all about form. There was nothing about substance. Surely that's the wrong way round?

I will accept your criticism if you promise to manage your board meetings in the way I suggest. Weak information, poorly managed meetings, and inadequate presentation can make a successful business look less good than it is. But of course, however neatly presented your information, however well-managed a board meeting, they cannot make a business successful if it is doing badly.

RELATIVE SUCCESS

One definition of a successful business is a relative one. A business which is beating budget is, by one measure, doing well.

Do you remember your business plan? In Chapter 3 we discussed the tightrope the entrepreneur needs to walk between fact and fiction. Fact does not always get backed, we agreed, but fiction can lead to friction.

In the first financial period after the investment is made, your budget will be drawn directly from your business plan. After all, you can hardly turn round to your new partner the morning after and say: "Thanks for the cash. I'll now rebudget the plan because, in all honesty, I bigged it up a bit so I could raise money from you." Your investor will start using worse words than the "oh shit" of the inaugural board meeting and you might even find yourself on the receiving end of one of those unheard-of warranty claims, on the basis that you did not prepare your business plan with due care and attention.

So let's hope that you followed the advice in Chapter 3 and made sure that the projections for the first period of the plan were relatively modest.

The trouble is that you will probably find yourself falling short of even this relatively modest plan. Out of my 23 companies I cannot think of one that overachieved against its first-year financial plan, except perhaps the one or two which projected no revenue at all and managed to spend money a little more slowly than they anticipated (because everything, including hiring and expenditure, happens more slowly than expected in Year 1).

Underperformance against the Business Plan in the first year seems an almost immutable law of nature. There are logical reasons for this. The funding round always takes longer to complete than anticipated. It always absorbs more management time than you expect. It consumes more energy, so that the completion of the funding round is often followed by a period of easing off, recharging batteries, even a vacation. When you turn your full attention back to the business it seems to take more time than you thought to step on the gas again, to make those key new hires, and to conclude the conversations with important early customers. One of the essential elements in any entrepreneur's make-up is the belief that his product or service is so compelling that it will be taken up fast. You have to be possessed by this optimism and enthusiasm to be crazy enough to set up a business, but it is then almost inevitable that you underestimate the time it will take to get going.

That is the bad news, but the good news is that an experienced Angel, Dragon, or Vulture should expect this slippage to happen and should be ready for it. So even if you feel a bit disappointed and shamefaced at falling short, you can take some comfort from the fact that you may not have fallen short of your new investor's real expectations.

What about Year 2? Do you have to stick to the original business plan budget? No, you don't, and you almost certainly should not. Year 1 hasn't got you to where your plan anticipated you to be at the start of Year 2. So you learn your lessons from Year 1. At the start of Year 2 your information is more current and your market intelligence more accurate. Of course, you take that into account and adjust your budget.

Unless your investor is very callow indeed, he will not bat an eyelid at this apparent change in your company's trajectory. The chances are that he will not even remember in detail what the business plan said about the Year 2 projections. He has lots of other numbers to carry around in his head. He is more likely to remember the destination – "We are trying to build a business worth $200 million" – than the precise way there.

What is more, it is in your Vulture's interests as much as it is in yours to have an achievable budget. "How are things going at Xcorp?" he may be asked by his managing partner. He'd like to be able to manage a nonchalant shrug and the smiling reply, "We're doing fine, thank you. Actually, we're a bit ahead of budget."

"Ahead of budget? That is good news. No need to have them on the agenda for Monday, then."

That is a nice conversation for a thrusting Vulture to have.

If he has to make the answer, "OK, really. They're a bit behind budget, but they're OK," the conversation will move in a far less comfortable direction.

"Behind budget, you say? That's a pity. What is the cash position like? You'd better put it on the agenda for Monday."

By the way, note the subtle change from "we" to describe the company that is ahead of budget to "they" if it's behind.

In the two conversations above, the company could be achieving the same absolute results. All other things being equal, it may be true to say that a business doing $5 million of revenue against a budget of $4 million is a more valuable business than one doing $5 million against a budget of $6 million. But I would go further than that and say that I would rather have a $5 million revenue business beating its $4 million budget than a $6 million revenue business falling short of its $7 million goal. Success is relative to the targets you set.

The ramifications of over- and underachievement reach beyond your Vulture and his relationship with his boss. Quite probably, your Vulture has to prepare quarterly progress reports on each of his portfolio companies for external advisory boards or fund investors – the precious limited partners we talked about in Chapter 2. These daunting individuals often receive so much data that they don't have time to do more than flick over the pages murmuring, "Oh dear, that one is behind," or "Good, good, ahead of budget." They might then go on to mutter, "Mmm, who's the investment director on that one? He seems to be doing a good job."

Your Vulture's status in his firm, and with his investors, will rise if his portfolio is seen to be performing well relative to expectations. That in turn will help your position. You too will be talked about favorably in partner and investor meetings. Your stock will rise. You will be left alone to run your business. If you want or need to access another round of funding, it will be easier for you.

The other important consideration is the impact that being ahead of budget will have on morale inside your own team. Everyone will feel that they are succeeding. And they will look forward to reaping the rewards of that success in their performance-linked bonuses (more is coming on the sticky subject of remuneration in the next chapter).

So in Year 2 and thereafter you have the opportunity to recalibrate. You have the opportunity to set a budget that you are sure you can beat. Do so. Why create an unnecessary rod for your own back?

Nevertheless, in my experience few businesses crack budgeting even in Year 2. Most entrepreneurs are still over-optimistic, expecting their customers to be as visionary and energetic as they are themselves. It always takes longer than you expect to communicate the passion and excitement you feel for your product. Corporate customers, even enthusiastic early adopters, are more bureaucratic than you think, and slower to move forward however powerful your value proposition. Consumers, even the geeks, take longer than you imagine possible to change the way they lead their lives and to enhance their existence by purchasing your offering.

However, by Year 3 the best companies are beating their plan – not by too much, because you don't want to have to put up with your investor director's jokes about soft budgets, and then have to fight violently to hold down your next year's plan to achievable levels and secure your team's bonus scheme. But the comparison column at the right of your management accounts is no longer contained in brackets, or qualified by a minus sign, or printed in red. And you may be able to afford that color printer for the accounts department, except that now your numbers are all in black you no longer really need it.

ABSOLUTE SUCCESS

There are two occasions when the absolute becomes more important than the relative in measuring success. One, of course, is at exit, when a real valuation is placed on your business and your hard work gets turned into capital (although, as you will see when we get to Chapter 12, the relative remains highly important).

The other is more immediate: it is when you are running out of cash. Ultimately you cannot consume more cash than you have. In a public corporation, under the harsh glare of quoted company investors, you may be punished if you do not deliver the level of profit your guidance has led shareholders to expect. In a private company, cash is far more important than profit. When you run out of cash is when you get found out.

So at some point in most businesses, you have to come up with a budget which shows you achieving cash flow breakeven. Unless, that is, you have a biotech business or similar, in that the game plan is to develop intellectual property and to sell the business before any real revenue has been generated.

Unfortunately, it is when the absolute becomes more important than the relative that many businesses come unstuck. This is because it is often the pressure to show a cash flow breakeven budget before the money runs out that causes an unrealistic plan to be adopted. It is at this point that you can fall into the worst position of all. You find yourself underachieving in relative terms against the unrealistic budget that your cash flow breakeven ambitions forced you to set. In absolute terms you are sliding toward the disaster that running out of cash will bring. Just when you need to look good, in order to maintain your investor's support and secure another injection of funds, you find yourself looking very bad indeed.

BAD HABITS

One of the dangers of raising investment capital for your business is that it can give you bad habits. The investment you raise gives you the luxury of making losses, or of consuming more cash than the business can generate, which, as we have just agreed, is the most important measure of all. So for a while you have enjoyed the luxury of ignoring the most fundamental principle of good business; namely, to bring in revenue that exceeds the costs you have to pay out. You may have become addicted to the venture capital drug which allows you to flaunt this basic business principle. If you have, you will have to undergo a very painful cold turkey before the day of reckoning arrives. I sounded a warning about this right back in Chapter 1.

The period when the cash well is running dry is obviously dangerous because it can spell the end of your business. It is also dangerous because it is when the control of the business potentially slips away from you and into the claws of your venture capital beast. He will typically become your lender of last resort. If you do not have an alternative plan, if you have to rely on additional investment to survive, your investor can pretty much dictate his own terms. The fact that he only owns 25% of your business is irrelevant. The fact that the Investor Rights Agreement or Shareholders' Agreement only gives him veto rights is equally irrelevant. You will have potentially allowed control of your business to slip through your fingers and you deserve to suffer whatever happens next.

ALTERNATIVE PLANS

Here is the *leitmotif* again. As I have already said many times in this book, make sure that you have an alternative plan. Do not allow wishful thinking to weaken your grip on reality. All too often I have seen management teams take the weak decision to postpone a crisis by setting an overoptimistic budget. Often they are aided and abetted in this criminal offense by their Angel, Dragon, or Vulture. Indeed, I have myself been an accessory after the fact more often than I like to admit.

My defense, and it is a weak one, is that it is the chief executive's job to run the business, and the non-executive director's job to ask questions and provide support. Many times I have sat in board meetings studying the delightful spreadsheeted budget which magically shows the company I have backed moving into cash flow breakeven before the money I have been responsible for investing runs out. My heart fills with excited relief – we are about to turn the corner – and with pride – I may have made a good investment. My head remembers that I have seen this many times before and forces reluctant words out of my mouth.

"Are you really sure that this is achievable? You don't often see companies like this quadrupling revenue year on year. A little bit of slippage in those two big orders, and we will be out of cash. And if one of them goes away completely, then... then we will be in a real mess."

Do I detect a slightly reproachful expression as the chief executive raises his eyes from studying the magic spreadsheet?

"Oh ye of little faith! Don't worry. The head of sales has personally qualified those leads. He thinks that they will come in two or three months sooner than we are budgeting. Anyway, the pipeline is pretty broad now; there will be other stuff moving forward in the unlikely event that they do slip. And it is not until halfway through the year, so we will have plenty of time to adjust if we need to. There is plenty of time to get a contingency plan together."

Perhaps the Vulture lets it go at that point. Perhaps he has a contingency plan of his own. Perhaps he is still excited enough about the prospects of the company to want to put more money "to work" in it. Perhaps he has sounded out his partners and knows that they will be receptive to approving an additional investment. Perhaps – and this is where the picture gets darker – he knows that when the company has its back to the wall he may be able to extract more attractive terms, or insist on some of the management changes for which he has been lobbying.

Let's rewind to the beginning of the reel and give the CEO a better script.

"So that first spreadsheet shows that there is a reasonable possibility that business will close early enough to carry us through to cash flow breakeven. I have focused the head of sales on qualifying the sales opportunities in the cash flow. And

I have also spent time with those customers myself. They really are looking quite promising, but I do not want to bet the business on them closing next quarter. There are other opportunities in the pipeline, but realistically they are further back.

"So I have worked on a cut-back budget. That is shown in the next spreadsheet. It is not very pretty, and it means that we will struggle ever to grow the business as we hoped. It will make it much harder to close those new customers because without most of our development team we will not be able to add some of the new product features they want. In the near term we would have to switch the techies back to doing some consultancy. But it does mean we will survive.

"The alternative would be to put a contingency funding plan in place now. Might you be able to commit to enough funding to buy us another six months before we have to make any overhead cuts? With some bridge funding in place from you we could set about talking to other new investors."

Because you are now firmly in control, as a chief executive should be, the Vulture is now more likely to go back to his investment committee with confidence. He can honestly say that you are doing a good job, that there is a good chance that the necessary new business will come in, but that you very wisely do not want to count on it. He will say that your budget proposal shows significant overhead reductions which will most probably damage the upside. "It is just not in our interests for that to happen," he will say. "It would be far better to extend the runway by putting in another $1 million. And it might be worth putting feelers out to a couple of other investors about joining us at this point."

REBUDGETS

Sometimes, partway through a financial year, expectations have been missed by a large margin. Maybe that is the fault of overoptimistic budgeting at the start of the year; maybe external circumstances have changed. Maybe that very reasonable assumption you made about a major new customer has proved wrong, or management changes at one of your existing customers have caused a previously reliable revenue stream to dry up. Should you soldier on, or should you recast the budget?

I have sat in board meetings where investors have advanced arguments both for and against. That surprises me, for in my mind there is absolutely never a doubt. One of the few advantages that a small business has over a large business is the ability to change direction quickly, to adjust as fast as necessary to new circumstances. So as soon as you believe that your budget is materially out of reach, replan, with the objective above all of getting your costs in line with what you can afford.

The important proviso here is that you should not lose sight of the budget you set at the beginning of the year. It is one thing to set a Year 2 budget which is less ambitious than shown in your original business plan. That is acceptable, even normal. It is quite another to have to replan partway through a financial year. Almost whatever the extenuating circumstances, you have to acknowledge an element of failure. You should learn a lesson yourself from the experience, and not congratulate yourself partway through the second half because you are meeting your replanned, reduced "budget."

You should also not run the unnecessary risk of making your Vulture sharpen his talons, of causing your Dragon to breathe fire, or of making your Angel turn devilish. If he finds that all reference to your original budget has suddenly disappeared from the management accounts, and that adverse variances have become positive as a result of the simple expedient of replacing one column of numbers with another, he may well feel – perhaps with some justification – that you are trying to pull the wool over his eyes. Vultures in particular use reporting systems for their partners and fund investors which are not necessarily easily adapted to a change in budget partway through a period. So by all means add your new budget to your own management reports, but leave the old one in place as well so that your outside directors and their colleagues can see exactly where you are against where you originally expected to be, without scrabbling back through their old files.

And as for resetting your bonus scheme along with your budget, don't even think about it. Which leads me neatly into the controversies of the next chapter.

CHAPTER NINE

Remuneration

It's only money...

He's given us a whole chapter on how to organize board meetings, and now he is planning a whole chapter on remuneration, I hear you complain. Why doesn't he tell me something interesting that I don't know about? Is he a Dickens, a Trollope, or a Balzac, being paid by the word? Aha. There – you *are* interested in remuneration. I rest my case. The chapter stays. But first, to make you feel better, let me put on record the cruel statistic that only 2% of writers earn more than $150,000 per annum, and 80% of us have to be satisfied with less than $30,000 annually.

Perhaps that is why people like authors more than bankers, bosses of large businesses, and politicians. Remuneration in public companies and public life seems to be the single topic that arouses more anger and outrage than any other among shareholders and the general public. More attention is paid to bankers' bonuses and their pensions than to what they actually do and the impact of their actions on our economic system. More interest is shown in the salaries and expenses of senators and members of parliament than in the laws that they pass.

So you should not be surprised to find that the single issue that is most likely to cause tension and disagreement between you and your Angel, Dragon, or Vulture is your remuneration.

In the good old days before you took investment it was simple. You could pay yourself as much as you liked if your business was doing well and generating enough cash to cover it. If it wasn't doing well and didn't have any cash, you might not be able to pay yourself at all.

In a sense that is the nub of the issue. On one level your Angel or Vulture has put money into your business so that your salary gets paid whether you are generating cash or not. From his point of view it is more than reasonable to demand some control over your remuneration now that it is being paid with his money. And even when you are profitable and generating cash again, a proportion of that cash effectively belongs to your outside shareholders, so they may be justified in feeling aggrieved if all that cash is used to pay management team bonuses.

Nevertheless, it can be galling suddenly to find that your remuneration is under scrutiny again. Why, it is almost like going back to being a salaryman, and to escape from that was one of the reasons you set up your business in the first place. Still, to avoid the issue becoming a running sore, you will have to put that thought behind you and understand how your investor is likely to think on this controversial subject.

JEALOUSY

One of the reasons everyone seems to take a prurient interest in what everyone else earns is the green-eyed monster. Why should he get more than me, when what I do is just as difficult and when I work just as hard? I could do what he does, and do it better. And so on.

It is worth thinking back to Chapter 2, and the financial position of your investors. Your Vulture, if you remember, has various pressures on what he earns. Some of this may just come from the size constraints of his own relatively small business. Management fees may not yet be high enough to cover a very generous level of salary. Or his investors, the limited partners, may have become limiting partners and may be eyeing salary levels with anxiety lest the general partner becomes rich on fees and does not have to bother too much with delivering good performance. Or the senior partners in the firm may be keeping their younger colleagues lean and hungry, either as a result of their own excessive appetites, or because they want to keep them energetic and trying hard for the end-of-year bonus.

Your Vulture is likely to feel these pressures close to his heart. They may be so close to his heart that he wants to impose the same pressures on you. His managing partner may well have said to him that it is fair enough for him to earn the going rate for doing the basic job. A strong annual performance, where he exceeds expectations, of course deserves to be rewarded with a decent bonus (still always bearing in mind market norms), but making serious money should rightly depend on making a significant capital upside for investors. You may feel that your Vulture is displaying a certain lack of imagination when he puts on his remuneration committee hat and repeats to you what his managing partner has said to him, and you may be right. But it is also human nature.

Your Angel, or your Dragon, does not have a senior partner breathing down his neck, but he may be thinking back to his own position when he was at a similar point in his own career. Because it was probably a little while ago, he was probably earning less than you, and this may color his judgment about what is reasonable.

PROCESS

By now you may know me well enough to appreciate that one of my many weaknesses is to talk about form first and substance second. So you will not be surprised if I tackle the process of reaching agreement about remuneration before moving on to remuneration itself.

In Chapter 5, when we touched on the terms of the Investor Rights Agreement or Shareholders' Agreement, we noted that one of the matters over which your investors would seek to exercise veto rights was remuneration. In part, we observed, this is to prevent all the value, whether in terms of cash or earnings, being stripped out of the business to the benefit of the executives and to the detriment of the outside shareholders.

These remuneration controls are typically exercised in one of two ways. One possibility is that the Vulture, Angel, or Dragon is simply given the right to approve all remuneration packages above a certain level; sometimes this threshold is set around $100,000 per annum, or £60–70,000, but sometimes it is set a lot lower. Typically this approval would be given by your personal Mephistopheles in his capacity as a non-executive director. The second possibility, more normal perhaps when a company has progressed further and when more than one investor is involved, is to set up a remuneration committee to deal with all aspects of rewards for board members and other senior executives. In these cases the remuneration committee – or remco for short – may be composed entirely of outside directors. If not, it will certainly have a majority of outside directors, including one or more representatives of the investors. The remco will consider proposals made by the chief executive, and will approve them or not, typically then making a report to the board and seeking the board's formal approval of its recommendations. As you can see, it quickly all gets a bit convoluted.

One of the worst things that can happen is for the process of agreeing rewards – for the team as a whole, but especially for the CEO – to develop into a negotiation between executive management and investors. This, in my experience, can only lead to ill-feeling and bitterness. So do not approach the process as a haggle, by going in higher than is reasonable and expecting to be pegged back. If you do, the investor director, or the members of the remco, will feel that you are trying to pull a fast one in an unreasonable way which ignores the rights of non-management shareholders. Aim to start with a reasonable package which will meet with easy approval. When that approval comes with ease, do not make the mistake of feeling that if you had started higher you might have got a little bit more. If you had started higher, your non-executive colleagues might have felt that you were being unreasonable and pushed back. By all means allow yourself the luxury of a little feeling of moral superiority, but remember that you have a reasonable solution, and that what really matters is building success and making a substantial return over the medium term. Save your hard negotiating skills for your customers.

SALARIES

Whereas in an owner-managed business you can pay yourself whatever you want, so long as the business can sustain it (but normally cannot pay yourself whatever you want because the business cannot sustain it), once you have outside shareholders you move closer to a regime which pays the going rate for the job. As you know, the going rate depends on a number of things: the size of the business, the sector in which it operates, its geographical location, and so on. But it may also depend on your own age, skills, and qualifications.

It may be an unpalatable fact that if you take all these things into account, your salary should by rights go down rather than up. You were doing well before you took investment, and so you were able to pay yourself generously, perhaps more generously than similar individuals in similar companies with different ownership structures. Most incoming investors will probably accept that it is not reasonable for your basic salary to go down when they come on board – "We want you to worry about running the business, not about how you are going to cover your living expenses" – but you may at least need to reconcile yourself to not receiving any annual increases until you are in line with the market outside. Some incoming investors may require that you move to the going rate as part of the price of their investment.

And how do you determine what really is the going rate? Executive search firms often have useful data, or produce salary surveys, and are worth cultivating. And the network of other CEOs which you built when you were doing due diligence on your potential Vulture, and which you have assiduously maintained, can be very useful. This *keiretsu* has the added advantage of being able to shed light on your investor's specific prejudices and preferences.

This is another moment when, if you do not have an independent chairman in place, you may wish fervently that you did. On a subject as inflammatory as remuneration, a wise intermediary can be invaluable. He can talk frankly to you, gather your views, and then sound out the investors. If he comes back with the intelligence that the investor will not go a cent over $200,000, and that to suggest $220,000 will just provoke a pointless argument, he will have gone a considerable way toward earning his own fees. You may feel that his position is even better justified by the information that the investor views $200,000 as the right level, when you were thinking of $180,000. I have known both happen.

As time goes on and you build your team, the picture can become more complicated. But first of all there may be another problem. It quite often happens that at the beginning of a business there are two equal partners. One might be focused on technology, say, and one on sales and marketing. When you set the business up together it was agreed that you would be on the same salary, and have the same equity stake. The trouble is, that was five years ago and things have moved on. Now your partner is still in charge of technology, but you effectively run the business. CEOs get more money than CTOs. So should your salary be adjusted upward? Or his downward? Or should you stick at the same level for old time's sake? How you resolve that sensitive issue will depend to an extent on your personal preference, but in an ideal world you should move to market rates if you can.

One of the main reasons for doing so is that as you build up the team, you have to try to bring its new members in on market rates. If the founders are themselves out of line it can make recruitment – an already challenging task – more challenging still. And not only is it a challenging task, but hiring the right people is the single issue that more than any other will determine whether or not you are successful. You do not want to make it any more difficult than it is already.

Quite often, if, as you should be, you are aiming to hire top-quality people with the right experience to help grow your business, you will be recruiting people who are already working for bigger businesses. Bigger businesses frequently equal bigger salaries. If you have not got your own scale right before tackling these new hires, you may find that either you end up paying too much, or that you cannot attract them. You may want to be able to justify hiring on lower basic salaries because of the capital upside offered; if your own salaries are higher than normal market rates you may not be able to do so. And if they are too low you may find yourself trying to pay too little and not getting the good people you need.

These problems can be especially acute if – or when – you are trying to bring in a new chief executive. Don't choke. I consider this sensitive subject more in the next chapter.

BONUS SCHEMES

Everyone seems to have their own preferred way of structuring bonus schemes. This should be an area where your Angel, Dragon, or Vulture has more experience than you, just because he will almost certainly have been involved with more businesses. Lean on him; learn from his experience.

My tips, from my experience, would be as follows:

1 Select the two most important goals for the company and base the bonus scheme on those (typically revenue and cash, early on anyway).

2 Keep it simple so that everyone can understand it and know what they stand to earn without needing to build a spreadsheet.

3 Have everyone in the team on the same goals, so that they work like a team.

4 Avoid cliffs: have the bonus scheme kicking in at 90% of budget, say, sliding up to full on-target earnings at budget, and rewarding overachievement up to 120% of budget. (If you have a cliff, and narrowly miss it, you will almost certainly end up having an awkward conversation about paying some of the bonus even though you have missed the goal.)

5 Do have a cap: too much overachievement in one year is not necessarily a good thing, because it then makes the next year more difficult and a steady growth progression harder to achieve. You do not necessarily want to incentivize your team (or yourself) to pull too much revenue artificially forward. Two things are important in building capital value: consistent growth from year to year and a reliable business model (sometimes known as a "high quality of earnings"). You want to be able to recognize revenue in as conservative a way as accounting standards allow, so that you can build up a bit of a reserve for a rainy day.

6 If you miss the goals, don't ask for some of the bonus to be paid out, however hard people have worked. If you're going to do that, you might as well not have a bonus scheme at all. It is meant to motivate and reward achievement. People are paid their salaries to work hard; they are paid their bonuses for success.

EXPENSES

When it was just your business, if you were doing quite well, maybe you put the occasional slap-up meal on expenses, or treated yourself to a business-class flight, or a taxi fare when you could have taken the bus. After all, it was a tax-efficient way of giving yourself a small pat on the back.

Once you have sold some of your equity and started to build a team, you will have to go back to the Spartan ways you followed when there was no cash in the bank. Your Angel, Dragon, or Vulture will respect frugality and suspect extravagance. Your example will be followed throughout the company; or, if there is one rule for you and one rule for the others, you will build up resentment and quickly destroy morale. To make yourself feel a bit better, you can also take pleasure from imposing the same rules about expenses on your investors.

When businesses I have been involved in have got into trouble and had to cut costs, it has always infuriated me if they say proudly that they have imposed a ban on unnecessary travel, found a way of buying air tickets more cheaply, or got a special deal on hotels. That is how large companies behave. Small companies should never allow unnecessary travel, they should never buy expensive air tickets, and they should never not get a special deal on hotels.

If you have just sold 25% of your business to raise $1 million, remember that spending $1,000 extra on an air fare is like spending an extra 0.025% of the value of your business. An extra $10,000 on expenses is 0.25% of the equity. $40,000 and you are talking about 1% – the same level of equity that you may be considering granting to some of your senior people.

EQUITY AND OPTIONS

That brings me on to the most difficult area of all. It is the most difficult area because it is potentially the most valuable, and thus the one that in financial terms matters most. It also probably matters most in emotional terms. Yet it is also the most clearly defined by finite barriers: there can only ever be 100 percentage points of equity. Awarding one individual a salary of $200,000 does not necessarily reduce his colleague's $200,000. But of course, giving one individual a 5% option grant does reduce his colleague's existing 5% – by 5% – and your own stake. It also reduces your Angel, Dragon, or Vulture's stake by 5%. So if you thought he was oversensitive in the salary and bonus discussion, just wait until you start discussing an increase in the size of the option pool with him.

Another problem with equity and options is the extra dimension they bring: the dimension of time. Salary and bonus are simple payments for work done in the current year. They are easily measurable, easily comparable, and easily quantifiable. Not so equity. The amount of equity held by different individuals in the team may well depend on whether they were founders of the business, or whether they joined early on. People joining at different points may have paid different prices for their shares, or they may be required to pay different prices in the future when they exercise their options. And the ultimate value of the equity is in any case uncertain.

It is quite possible that Gary, that engineer who joined the company early on and did some important work on the core technology, holds more equity, or options, than Andrea, the head of development, hired in as Gary's boss in Year 3. Maybe Gary even earned some additional equity because he agreed to work for a sub-market salary during those difficult early months when there wasn't enough cash in the business. So part of Gary's equity is his by right because he effectively paid for it out of his salary. Andrea, on the other hand, was granted options at the market price when she joined, on the basis that she should benefit from her contribution to the increase in the company's future value. Or was Andrea's option grant made partly because she agreed to join at a lower salary than she was earning before? Maybe there's a element of "salary sacrifice" about Andrea's options, as with Gary's equity.

And how should the good leaver/bad leaver rules that we discussed with such trepidation in Chapter 5 influence all this? Is it fair for Gary to be made to sell his shares (including those that he earned from salary sacrifice) if he gets fed up with working for Andrea and leaves? Or if Andrea decides that Gary's lack of discipline and tiresome inability to document his work mean that there is no longer a place for him in the structured development team that Andrea has been hired to build? Anyway, nobody can quite remember why Gary was given those shares in the first place. The corporate documentation in those early days was no better than Gary's is now. And why has he got some options as well as some shares? Should they be treated in the same way? Does he mind? He's an engineer after all; does he really understand what an option is?

The permutations are endless, and the opportunities myriad for seeding disenchantment where the intention was to sow motivation. And in case this was not complicated enough on its own, you will find out that different investors have different views about what is fair, or what is not, and what the purpose is of issuing equity and granting options. And this is then compounded by variations in custom and practice between geographies. If you find yourself with Americans and British members on your board, they may have very different views about how the option scheme should work. Finally, the tax man has to put in his oar, because the fiscal treatment of equity and options varies in different jurisdictions, adding to the pressure of what you should do to give your scheme the most effective motivating power.

Ultimately, in my view, there is no single right way to organize the equity and option element of your remuneration policy. Many debates at many board meetings have convinced me that there are umpteen perfectly valid approaches. But there are just as many wrong ways of doing it. One good way to avoid those, and to retain clarity about what you are trying to achieve and why certain policy decisions result from this, is to write down in simple terms the objectives and the concomitant rules. These should be shared openly with employees when grants are being made, along with a clear explanation of how options work and what they might be worth if the company achieves its goals.

The ignorance with which options are often reported in the media always bewilders me. Some newspapers still publish articles that seem designed to whip up public outrage that the CEO of A Corporation has been awarded $10 million in share options. That number of $10 million is based on the cost to the CEO of A Corporation of exercising his options, not on what the options might be worth to him. I have known this misleading media reporting infect employee option holders in unquoted companies and confuse them about the value of their own options, to the point where options with a higher exercise price become more precious than those with a lower exercise price, which of course are really the more valuable ones.

If the objectives and rules are laid before investors during their due diligence process, a useful debate can be held and any differences of view resolved at that point.

So let me have a stab at a set of objectives:

1 The objective of Xcorp's remuneration policy is to fairly reward and thereby motivate employees.
2 Remuneration is made up of four principal elements: salary, bonus, equity, and options.
3 Salary provides an immediate recompense for the job being done to the best of an employee's ability.

4 A bonus provides an additional incentive to succeed in the current financial period, and a reward for success.

5 Shares are held by founders and early members of the company, according to their respective roles in starting the company, the amounts they invested, and the risks that they took when the business was starting up.

6 Equity has also been bought by outside investors in order to fund the development of the company. Additional equity may be sold for the same purpose in the future.

7 The option scheme offers a reward and an incentive over the medium and longer term by enabling newer employees to acquire shares in the company. An option gives its holder the right to acquire a certain number of shares at future dates at a specified price; it therefore has no readily realizable value until there is a market in the shares and the shares resulting from the option exercise can be sold.

That is the relatively easy and uncontroversial bit. Now we move into areas where there are many possible permutations. Here is one possible set of rules.

The main principles governing the option scheme are as follows:

1 Options will be not granted until an employee has been with the company for six months.

2 Options will be exercisable at the fair market value prevailing at the date of grant.

3 Options do not vest and may not be exercised until three years after the date of grant.

4 If the optionholder's employment ceases, vested options may be exercised within 30 days, but all other options will lapse.

5 If the optionholder's employment ceases, any shares acquired as a result of previous option exercises must be

sold back to the Company at the prevailing fair market value, in accordance with the Certificate of Incorporation or the Articles of Association.

6 If the company is acquired, half the optionholder's unvested options will become exercisable. The company will use its reasonable endeavors to negotiate the roll-over of the remainder into the acquirer's own option scheme.

7 If the company lists its shares on a public stock exchange, no changes to the terms of the options will be made, except that the exercise of options and the trading of any resultant shares will be subject to the normal trading rules of the stock exchange in question.

Most of these rules are subject to as many permutations as there are rules. Let me take them one by one and try to explain the thinking (the tax rules I've used are those in the UK, but the argument is equally applicable elsewhere).

CONVERSATIONS WITH A VULTURE (ON OPTIONS)

SCENE 1: ELIGIBILITY FOR OPTION SCHEME

"I won't be able to recruit unless people can qualify for the option scheme immediately. Those options are a key part of the remuneration package and we need to get the pricing clock ticking."

"Maybe that's right," concedes the Vulture, "with senior guys anyway. Are you just going to have senior guys in the scheme, or are you going to extend it to everyone, even the secretaries?"

"I like the idea of making everyone eligible. It would create more of a team spirit."

"I don't know about that. When the junior guys do the math they'll work out how little their options will ever be

---

worth, and that can be a real turn-off. They probably won't understand what an option is anyway. And if they do decide to leave that's no real downside for us. There is only a finite number in the pool. Ultimately it's your call, but if it were me I'd keep them in reserve for the senior guys – the ones who'll value the options, who'll really make a difference, who'd hurt us if they left. And if you think I'm going to approve an extension of the pool above 10% you've got another think coming."

SCENE 2: THE EXERCISE PRICE

"I know we have to set the strike price at fair market value when the options are granted. We don't want to crystallize a tax liability up front. But I've heard that you can create a new class of share that comes behind the preference stack or has weaker rights than the others to get the tax authorities to agree a low valuation. I want to get it as low as possible. And if we can get the senior guys' options all within the £100,000 limit for the EMI (Enterprise Management Incentive), that would be even better. Then they'll just pay capital gains tax on everything. Anything we can't get in the EMI will cost 40%, or even 50%, and that is before the National Insurance."

The Vulture looks thoughtful. "Sure, I don't like people paying unnecessary tax." He pauses and shakes his head. "But why should we grant options at a low price? After all, making money on the options is meant to be an incentive for increasing the value of the company from here. With a strike price below our investment price, we'd be rewarding them for failure, for reducing the value of our shares. They might make money while we were still losing it."

"But we will have to grant fewer options because we'll make the same amount of money with fewer shares, so you will get less dilution. If each option is worth more, we'll have to grant fewer."

"Oh yeah? And what about the increase in valuation our company gets because of the additional cash in the balance sheet from the option exercise? If you ask me, the lower dilution from granting fewer options – theoretical anyway – is balanced out by the reduced proceeds of the lower exercise price."

"I haven't sold a company before, but I bet that gets lost in the wash."

"Well maybe, sometimes. But it shouldn't be. After all, cash is cash."

SCENE 3: THE VESTING PERIOD

"Why should an employee have to wait three years before any of their options vest?" you ask.

"Because it makes them a better retention instrument. They'll have to stay for at least three years then," responds the Vulture.

"But that's unfair, because they're effectively part of their salary. They should vest on a straight-line basis over three years. No, two years."

"What if they vest in three equal amounts after one year, two years, and three years?" insists the Vulture.

"No, that's unfair too – there's still a cliff and if they leave one day short of two years they lose a third of their options."

"But that's the point: we want them to stay with the company." And so on.

SCENES 4 AND 5: IF THE OPTIONHOLDER LEAVES

"I told you she would leave," sneers the Vulture.

"That's because you attached so many strings to the options that she thought they weren't worth anything."

"She's got 30 days to exercise them."

"But then she has to sell them back to the company at FMV."

"So? She'll make what she deserves to make. She has contributed to a modest increase in value, that's all. Why should she get the benefit of everyone's work over the next three years to exit? And the last thing you want is to have a lot of ex-employees wandering around as small shareholders. If we ever get to exit it's a nightmare, let me tell you."

SCENES 6 AND 7: ACCELERATED VESTING ON EXIT

"So why shouldn't all the options vest on exit? After all, that is mission accomplished."

"First of all, why should someone join just six months before and benefit from a windfall? How is that fair on the others? Secondly, what do you think the company that acquires us is buying? They want our people. If they see them all getting fat option pay-offs, they will be worried about them all leaving. They need to roll over into the acquirer's own scheme."

"But what if they don't want all my team? What if they are fired? Shouldn't they be able to exercise if they aren't wanted?"

"Well, we could go for a 'double trigger' mechanism."

Blank look.

"That's where if you are bought, and then fired within six months, you get to exercise all your options. Nah, too complicated, because you never know how many more will exercise and you need an escrow and so on."

"And if we IPO?"

"No way can we have acceleration on IPO. No way."

TRANSPARENCY

The best practical test of your remuneration policy is whether you are able to be utterly open about it or not. You need to expect that salaries, bonuses, equity, and options will all be discussed among friends in the company. If there are anomalies, or if there appear to be anomalies, they are likely to emerge and to cause ill-feeling. It is far better to be deliberately transparent and to encourage a culture of openness about remuneration.

If you feel uncomfortable exposing to your colleagues what you earn, or how much of the company you own, then it can only be because in your heart of hearts you know that you're being greedy. If you're receiving a fair reward for your work in the company that you founded, you should be able to be open about it. And if you're not, you should make some adjustments, because the likelihood is that you will ultimately make less than you might have made because you will have been breeding discontent in your team.

ACCURACY

Conversations about remuneration often take place one on one or in small huddles. In the early days, it might be a conversation between the Angel/Dragon/Vulture and the CEO in the corridor or lobby. Later on, even when there's a structured remuneration committee, it tends to be a less formal meeting than the board, and the normal board minute taker is often not present. Far too frequently, the all-important discussion about the bonus scheme, or about the options, is tacked on at the end of a board meeting, when time has run out and people need to get away, added to which are the complexity of some of the issues and the many possible different points of view. The conversations above may make nothing clear except for the difficulties and the possibilities for disagreement, but I hope at least that they make those plain.

Very often, in my experience, what is decided about remuneration is not remembered clearly, or is remembered differently by different participants in the conversation. Equally important, *why* things are decided in a particular way is frequently forgotten. Then, half the time, the necessary administration is not completed: the application to the tax authorities for approval of the option exercise price is overlooked, or the issue of the option certificate itself. Few young businesses have a separate human resources function. Often these matters fall in the CFO's lap, yet often he is not party to all these discussions.

Earlier in this chapter I urged you to record in plain English the principles guiding your remuneration policy, and to make sure that they are agreed by everyone with an interest in making them work. Also make sure that when decisions are taken, they are properly minuted, those minutes approved by all the stakeholders, and the follow-up admin completed on the same basis. Otherwise what the policy is and what has been agreed will be forgotten. Then there will be tension and argument.

For a moment put yourself in the Vulture's nest: he will most likely be grappling with these issues in several companies, all doing things in a slightly different way. Unless you record what has been agreed, he will mix up conversations and become confused, and you will become irritated and aggrieved. The problems that I come to in the next chapter will be unnecessarily exacerbated and you will blunt the main tool you have for managing your most valuable asset – your people.

CHAPTER TEN

People

Management, management, management

I remember once participating on a panel at a venture capital conference at London Business School. The room was hot and airless. The discussion was dull and bland. The eyelids of the audience were drooping. Even the chairman of the panel had to stifle a yawn as he threw it open to the floor for questions.

"What are the three most important things you look for in a new investment?" came a voice from the back of the room. The chairman turned to the panelist at the end of the row furthest from me. I tried to stifle a yawn too. I knew what the answer was going to be.

"The first thing is good management. The second thing is good management. And the third? The third is good management too." A smile played smugly on the panelist's rubbery lips, off which the comfortable mantra had rolled.

The guy on his left did not have much to add. "Yup," he reiterated, "that's right. It's all about management, management, and management."

His neighbor would have liked to say the same, but was forced to expand a bit. "You see, if you've got a good team, not only will they run the business well, but they are unlikely to be in a bad business in the first place."

I shifted forward in my seat as my turn came. I had to say something different. I cleared my throat.

"I am sorry, but I disagree with my colleagues here. I take a different view." One or two of the nodding heads in the audience snapped upright. Could this be a welcome moment of controversy? "We're talking about early-stage venture capital here. So I look first for the market opportunity. Then I look to see whether the company has the right technology, or the potential to develop the solution to address that opportunity. Maybe management is the third element. But one of the things we try to do to help the companies we back is to bring in the right management. So if they are not in place on day one, we're not scared off. We add value by trying to find the right people."

The rest of the panel looked slightly startled. The chairman seemed a bit taken aback. "Do you have anything you want to add?" he asked the questioner at the back of the room.

"Well, just one comment. You see, I asked the same question at Stanford Business School a couple of weeks ago. Most of the panel said the same thing, but one of the partners from Sequoia – Mike Moritz, I think it was – said the same as that last guy here."

Yes! Score! I had certainly got that one right. The legendary Mike Moritz had backed Yahoo!, Paypal, Google, YouTube, and one or two other modest little successes. The other panelists eyed me enviously and I floated around on a cloud for the rest of the day.

Of course having good management is vital to the success of a company. But companies go through several phases in their journey from start-up to success, and it is highly unusual to find all the necessary skills in place at the very beginning. The skills needed in the early days tend to be very different from the skills later on. Not many entrepreneurs, especially first-time entrepreneurs, have the full range of talent to take their business from the start all the way to the finish. Not many later-stage CEOs have the early-stage bull-headedness to get a start-up off the ground.

Way back at the beginning of this book I cited an unsettling statistic, indeed so unsettling that I said it might make entrepreneurs want to stop reading at that point. Let me remind you.

In my venture capital career, I backed and sat on the board of 23 companies. Only 7 of those companies still had their original chief executive at the end of the journey; 5 of the 23 companies went bust. Strikingly, 4 of those 5 failures still had their original CEO. Here is the table from the introduction, to save you from thumbing back to it.

Company outcome	CEO changed	%	CEO unchanged	%	Total	%
Survivors	15	94	2	43	18	78
Failures	1	6	4	57	5	22
Total	16	100	7	100	23	100

For the purposes of this chapter, allow me to orient the table the other way round to show a different perspective on the percentages.

Company outcome	Survived	%	Failed	%	Total	%
CEO changed	15	83	1	20	16	78
CEO unchanged	3	17	4	80	7	22
Total	18	100	5	100	23	100

So of the 18 survivors and successes, 83% – 5 in 6 – changed their leadership. On the other hand, 80% of the failures – 4 in 5 – had the same leader in place. The sample is too small, and the other variables too significant, to conclude statistically that with a change in leadership you have an 80% chance of success, and without a change in leadership you have an 80% chance of failure. But at the very least it should make you think.

And every single one of those companies, of course, went through the process of building and expanding their team below board level. And then often the process of reducing it again, of reshaping and rebuilding once more.

Hiring the right people, at the right time, is often the most challenging element of building a business. It often bears the greatest risk. So to that extent, the other panelists at the London Business School were right; certainly they might have been right if the question had been: "What are the three main determinants of success?"

CAN YOU BEAR TO BRING IN YOUR OWN REPLACEMENT?

One of the first things you need to decide before you raise capital and accept outside investment is whether running your company and continuing to run your company until the exit is a *sine qua non* for you. If you decide that it is, and this is the first time you have done it but you still cannot contemplate any circumstances in which you would willingly hand over the reins, think, think, and think again before you take in external investment. Go back to Chapter 1 and reread it.

If you have built a business successfully before, or if you have been through the venture capital process as a founder, then your self-confidence may be justified. Then it is different. You may have the necessary experience, or just the right talents and the flair. You may be one of those semi-divine beasts about which I will talk in Chapter 13: the serial entrepreneur. If you are, you should probably be writing this chapter, not me.

However, if you are a first timer, and you decide that you are going to raise money, and you are determined to stay in the CEO role throughout, just remember that based on my small sample you have a one in six chance of doing so successfully. Maybe your self-confidence and your belief in your own ability are justified. Maybe you just need to see a good shrink, or to have your ego shrunk.

Bill Gates had not run a business before Microsoft. Maybe you're like Bill Gates, but don't count on it. I remember in 1998 that a certain internet industry guru compared one of the youngest entrepreneurs I ever backed to the great man. "He reminds me of the young Bill Gates," she said. Fortunately he was smart enough to take this compliment with a wide grin and a large pinch of salt, and did not try to remain as CEO of his company all the way through. Nevertheless, I don't think her flattery did him any favors.

Being determined to carry the ball all the way is a brave, high-risk strategy. Sometimes it works, and you get down the field for a glorious, spectacular touchdown. More often than not, you crash to the ground under a painfully crunching tackle, and soon after get hauled off the field by the coach. Then you get hauled over the coals for blowing that great scoring opportunity by refusing to pass the ball to the other player who was positioned so much better than you.

If you do decide that you're going to hang on to your role as CEO at all costs and things don't work out, you need to be prepared for an agonizing day of reckoning. If the money in the company has almost run out, and effective control of the business has passed away from you to your Angel, Dragon, or Vulture, you may face a bruising conflict and a very unhappy outcome. Your investors may well may demand management changes as a pre-condition for any new money. If you try to face them down, the company you founded may fail, and your chances of resuscitating it with outside money – or of raising outside money for another business in the future – will be extremely slim. If you accept your investor's terms, it will be hard for you psychologically and practically to keep a role in the business, and you may have to reconcile yourself to seeing what you started being finished by somebody else without your involvement.

You may think that your team will be loyal and will not accept another leader. You are probably in for an unpleasant surprise: they may actually welcome your replacement, because they may in fact believe, like your investors, that a change is necessary, indeed long overdue. They are in the best position of all to get an unimpeded view of your weaknesses.

And then maybe you will regret not paying more attention to those good leaver/bad leaver conditions I covered in Chapter 5. Or maybe they become irrelevant in themselves, because the refinancing to which you are forced to agree results in dilution which dramatically reduces the value of your residual holding anyway. Not many founder CEOs make much money if they are forced out of their companies because they have not been able to make them work.

There is of course an alternative: to accept at the very beginning that you might not have all the skills to take your company all the way. An open discussion with your potential Angel, Dragon, or Vulture should take place before invest-ment. Some founder CEOs hesitate to raise the subject. It is difficult, sensitive, emotional, and possibly embarrassing. Will the Vulture see it as sign of weakness, they think, if I express my view that I might not have the full set of skills or experi-ence, or that there are gaps in my team which will need filling in due course?

Not at all. If the Vulture you are talking to is any good at his job, he will see it as a sign of strength. If you do not raise the subject with him, he should raise it with you. If he does not raise it with you, then you should ask yourself whether he really understands what it takes to build a business. The Vulture may be burning to do the deal and invest in your com-pany. He may be anxious that if he raises the possibility that you might not be the right CEO for the duration you will go and take money from an investor who keeps quiet about it – at least until after the deal is done. By the way, if you do take money from someone like that, without addressing the leader-ship issue, you deserve what you get.

However, the venture capital beast can be more subtle. He should at least ask: "How do you see your team developing as the company progresses? What do you see as the strengths and weaknesses now? What gaps do you think you will need to fill and when? And where do you fit yourself in all that?"

If you say *ab initio* that you have not built a business like this before (something the investor will of course know anyway from your CV) and that you can see the time when it might be necessary to recruit someone into your own role, you are more likely to be extending your own tenure than shortening it, because you are demonstrating that you are a mature, sensible individual who is aware of the challenges ahead. And you are certainly making it more likely that you will find a satisfactory berth under the new CEO when that person is recruited.

THE DEVIL YOU KNOW, AND THE DEVIL YOU DON'T

It was easy to write that last little phrase, "when that person is recruited," but it hides myriad difficulties and risks. Any senior recruitment is difficult, expensive, and takes time. Recruiting a CEO is especially difficult, not least because it is so important. There is also a high risk that the individual you recruit will not cut the mustard. You may find after a significant period of disruption that he actually does the job less well than you, or at least certain important aspects of the job less well than you. You may find that you have to replace your replacement, and it is not unheard of for the founding CEO to step back into the role he gave up. But generally, the devil you know is no better than the devil you don't – you just don't want a devil at all.

YOUR OWN NETWORK

The nineteenth-century British statesman Benjamin Disraeli created an interesting character in his three novels *Sybil*, *Coningsby*, and *Tancred*: the fabulously wealthy Monsieur de

Sidonia, the greatest merchant banker of the age. In those days merchant bankers were almost venture capitalists. In a strange interlude halfway through *Tancred*, a flashback story is told of how Sidonia once met a group of talented traveling performers, the Baroni family. He likes them; he discerns in them great abilities; he finds them all far greater roles more worthy of their talents; one becomes an opera singer, one a ballet dancer, one a great actress, one a secret agent. This is how Disraeli describes Sidonia's approach to talent:

> *Sidonia had already commenced that habit which, during subsequent years, he has so constantly and successfully pursued, namely, of enlisting in his service all the rare talent which he found lying common and inappropriate in the great wilderness of the world, no matter if the object to which it might apply might not immediately be in sight. The conjuncture would arrive when it would be wanted. Thus he generally had ready the right person for the occasion; and, whatever might be the transaction, the human instrument was rarely wanting.*

No small business can enjoy the total luxury of Sidonia's approach. Nevertheless, it is possible to follow his example by making preparations for recruitment well in advance. Even if you cannot always secure talent when it is available, you can earmark it. Sometimes your Vulture genuinely can help: his network may produce a good candidate, or at least ensure that you avoid a bad one. But I have often found that Angels are better at avoiding devils and finding good candidates, because they will tend to have had longer careers, and therefore tend to have worked with more people over the years, and to have a wider network that might produce good candidates.

One lesson that small businesses can learn from Sidonia, though, is to grab talent if you see it, even if it is a little too early. So if you find a suitable CEO six months before you ideally want to step down, grab him while you can. If he's any good, he will no longer be available when the perfect time arrives.

INTERNAL RECRUITMENT

One of the advantages big businesses have over small is that they have a large internal talent pool of known individuals from whom they can pick. It is hard but not necessarily impossible for a small business to replicate this approach. One of the best CFOs I have worked with, for example, initially joined the company concerned in order to research and make acquisitions, having acted previously as an external adviser. Admittedly, that company was well past the start-up phase and had completed its IPO at that point. Acquiring a CEO in this way is especially difficult, but it can be done. That same company shuffled its pack twice and found excellent new CEOs from within its own ranks. It is perhaps no accident that the company, Surfcontrol, was the most successful investment I ever made, and returned 50 times cost to the first funds I invested in it.

One lesson that I have learned, forgotten, and then learned again is that when opening up a distant geographical territory, recruiting an unknown foreign national to fulfill this vital role is almost certain to end in failure. For European companies this challenge normally comes when addressing the North American market. In many areas of technology North America, or specifically the US, is both the largest market and, perhaps more importantly, the source of most innovation. So to be successful it is often necessary for European companies to address this market early, much earlier in fact than they really want to. In contrast, US technology companies often have the luxury of being able to leave Europe and Asia alone until they have built a strong presence in their home market. Frequently if European companies do so in reverse, they find that a strong local competitor has been established in the US and will overtake them. With the burgeoning innovation, especially in technology hardware, in Asia, the geographical rules may shift but the same principles will apply.

In my experience, the only way in which you can hope to tackle an overseas market successfully is to take a trusted existing employee from your home base and give him or her the job of establishing the overseas operation. It is almost impossible to attract genuine local talent to a foreign start-up, and equally impossible to check out whether they really are talent and get underneath their personal marketing skills. Therefore, take a suitable member of your team and use him or her to set up your overseas outpost. Then the culture will be aligned, the communication channels will be clear even across time zones, and you will not end up with two separate companies fighting each other. Often this is best done by one of your co-founders, but if none is available, at least plan ahead and hire someone into your local team whom you can groom for the overseas role.

HIRING SUCCESSFULLY

Maybe, just maybe, you will get lucky and find in your network, or your Angel's, Dragon's, or Vulture's network, the perfect candidate at just the right time to step into your shoes. Unfortunately, the chances are that you will find yourself hiring a headhunter to handle the recruitment for you.

My experience of recruiting senior management for portfolio companies in general, and CEOs in particular, has been that a success rate of much more than two out of three is hard to achieve. Thus you may want to ignore the rest of this section and perhaps you can do better without my advice.

For better or for worse, here are my dos and don'ts:

❑ Do ask each member of the board separately to write down all the necessary and desirable characteristics of the individual you are aiming to recruit.

❑ Do discuss these lists carefully in a board meeting and assemble a definitive specification.

❑ Don't simply eliminate all the controversial characteristics and go for the lowest common denominator.

❑ Do interview several headhunting firms and seek their views on your specification.

❑ Do select a firm that really understands your sector and companies of your size and stage and that really wants your business.

❑ Do careful reference checking on the headhunters, including with some people who are not on their own list of referees.

❑ Don't penny pinch about their fees: excessive negotiation on fees may mean they cut corners, and going with the cheapest for the sake of saving money will be a false economy. This recruitment may be the most important decision you ever take and you want the best people working on it with you, regardless of what they cost. If that hurts, remember it is your Angel/Dragon/Vulture's money anyway.

❑ Do make sure that the individual in the headhunting firm who pitches to you successfully is the person who will do all the work on your job bar the basic research. Often, especially in the large firms, the star performers are the ones who do the selling, and a faceless team back in the office carries out the assignment.

❑ Do make sure that the headhunter's fees are heavily weighted to success.

❑ Do listen to the headhunter's advice about the package that will be needed to attract an individual of the caliber you specify, but remember that it makes their job easier if the package is overgenerous.

❑ Do appoint one of your board to lead the recruitment process (ideally that chairman of yours).

❏ Do define the recruitment and the decision-making process clearly.

❏ Don't lead the process of recruiting your successor yourself. You will find it awkward, the candidates will find it awkward, and the relationship between you and the new CEO will get off to the wrong start.

❏ Do have the same three board members interview each candidate, take notes, and compare their notes together afterward.

❏ Do be one of these, and interview each candidate yourself.

❏ Do remember that you are selling the opportunity to join your company as much as candidates are selling themselves to you.

❏ Do make sure that all the interviewers (especially the Vulture) remember this.

❏ Do ask your three short-listed candidates to make a formal presentation to the whole board about their vision for the company and how they would run it.

❏ Do some of the reference checking yourself.

❏ Do make sure that you take up references with people who are not on the candidate's own list.

❏ Do talk to seniors, juniors, and peers.

❏ Do track down somebody you would expect to see on the candidate's reference list but who is not there (his last boss, for example).

❏ Don't think that you will find a candidate who is 100% of what you want.

❏ Don't hire somebody you feel uncertain about (yes, there is a contradiction between this point and the previous one).

❏ Don't be rushed into recruiting someone.

❏ Don't delay once you have decided to recruit your successor (yes, there is also a contradiction between this point and the previous one).

❏ Don't let anyone outside the board know that you're recruiting your successor (do you want to be a lame duck?).

- ❏ Don't let the other members of the board think that your negative feelings toward all the candidates are because you secretly want to go on doing the job.
- ❏ Don't waste money on psychometric testing unless you set great store by that sort of thing (if you're unsure whether the candidate is a nutter or not, don't hire him).
- ❏ Do trust your gut instincts.

MEANWHILE... DO NOT PUT OFF IMPORTANT DECISIONS

The recruitment process is itself fraught with risks and difficulties. There is a great temptation to compound them by putting off decisions which need to be made until the recruitment is completed.

Say you suspect that your head of sales is not performing. Do not fall into the trap of saying to yourself that maybe the new CEO will have the skills to coach him or manage him better. Do not fall into the trap of saying that you will delay recruiting a replacement until the new CEO is on board so that he can get his own person. It will take at least six months to get your new CEO. It may then take him three months to get his feet under the table. Then another three months for him to find the new head of sales. Before you know it, your decision not to deal with the current head of sales has cost you a whole year.

Equally, do not postpone a necessary round of cost reductions, or a new funding round. To do so could be to doom your business. While you are in charge, you have to keep on doing your job as well as you can. The chances are that the CEO you recruit will broadly endorse the decisions you and your board have made. If not, you may have got the wrong candidate. Again, trust your instincts.

AFTER RECRUITMENT

After you have hired your successor, and done the big thing in stepping back into a subsidiary role and accepted an outsider's authority, continue to trust your instincts. After the new CEO comes on board, it is natural for your own communication with your Angel, Dragon, or Vulture to reduce. After all, it is the CEO's role to communicate with the investors. A new relationship is developing and it would be wrong to get in the way.

Nevertheless, remember that you are in a better position than your outside board members to observe how the new CEO is performing. If you think that something's going wrong, do talk to your investors about it, perhaps through the invaluable medium of your chairman. Of course, there's a danger that your Vulture attributes your comments to sour grapes, or to an inability to let go. But if he's wise, he will listen to you. In fact, if he is doing his job properly, he should be reaching out regularly to you to test your views about how things are going under the new regime. It is false loyalty to say that everything in the garden is rosy when it is not. It is far better to express reservations if you have them. That can translate into useful coaching for the new incumbent, to the benefit of all concerned. Or, if the worst comes to the worst, it can result in a mistaken recruitment being identified quickly and being unraveled before too much damage is done.

And if your Vulture is doing his job properly, he will have made sure that he has other channels of communication into the company via which he can test your views. It is still very difficult for him to get it right and he may well need some help.

By now, I suspect you expect me to say it. Yes, it is the chairman *leitmotif* again. A good chairman will perform an invaluable role in helping to pick the right variety of CEO for a sunny aspect, in planting them firmly, watering them in, pruning them at the right time, and if necessary pulling them up again and popping them on the compost heap.

FIRING YOUR CO-FOUNDER

Those are three very brutal words. But if you are prepared to contemplate the possibility that you are not the right person to lead your business all the way, you have to be prepared to contemplate the possibility that your co-founder will not complete the whole journey in his original role either. You won the Vulture's respect, and he won yours, when you talked together at the beginning about the possibility that the right time might come for you to step down, or out. You should have the same conversation with your co-founder when you're discussing whether or not to raise outside funding. You should be open about what the implications might be. You should get him to read this book too. Buy him a spare copy (that's marketing, by the way). In the same way that you have taken on some of the onus to say when you think the time is right to change your own role, you should put some of the same responsibility on your co-founder.

Just as with your own role, if you let things run on unsatisfactorily for too long, you are making it less likely that a suitable alternative can be found, and ultimately you are doing your old friend a disservice.

BENEFIT OF THE DOUBT

I have heard it said that Vultures are far too eager to make management team changes when things are not going well. As soon as the company goes off budget, people say, they reach for the knife and plunge it between your ribs, or they take up the pistol and squeeze the trigger.

In my experience the absolute opposite is the case. Most investors wait too long before making management changes. I include myself in that. My worst mistakes have been in delaying that difficult conversation with the CEO for too long. Every single time I have been involved in making a change, I have regretted not doing it sooner. The best businesses I have been involved with have surprised – and sometimes even alarmed – me by coming and telling me that they want to make a change sooner than I expect.

It is human nature when you have backed someone to give them the benefit of the doubt. But by doing so you actually do a disservice to the person you want to be nice to.

Don't make the same mistake with your team. Generally, if someone shows they are not up to the job and performs poorly in one quarter, they are not going to pull themselves round in the next. One of the key skills of good management is to act as soon as one of your team is falling behind. By all means give them some mentoring and a chance to correct themselves. Tell them nicely but firmly where they are falling short, and what they need to do. Maybe even get them a short spell of training. By all means hope that they turn themselves around, but begin to get your contingency plan in place. The chances are that you will need it.

Round Two, and Three, and Four

Seconds out

The world might have a different view of the British sense of fair play if the Marquis of Queensbury had drafted his rules of boxing to allow a new participant to join in against the defending champion at the beginning of each new round. Suddenly, at the beginning of Round 2, you find yourself fending off punches from two opponents, one of them fresh. Then at the start of Round 3 you find another one trying to thump you. By Round 4 the ring is distinctly crowded and the fight more one-sided than ever.

Some chief executives could be forgiven for thinking that this is just what happens as each new funding round takes place, and as new opponents seem to appear. But then, depending on the circumstances, there may also be some low blows exchanged between the new combatants. This is not necessarily in your interests, although it can at least provide temporary, and perhaps comic, relief.

ACLAND'S LAW AGAIN

In Chapter 4 I formulated Acland's Law. If you remember, it stated that the complexity and difficulty of each round of funding with new investors can be expressed by the formula x to the power of y, where x is the first round and y is the number of each subsequent round. The conclusion, therefore, was to keep the first round simple. With your second round of investment comes the test of the extent to which you achieved that.

WHY LET ANOTHER PUGILIST INTO THE RING ANYWAY?

There goes the *leitmotif* again. Of course you need to have a fall-back plan which avoids any dependency on raising another funding round. But let's take that as a given. Why, if it is so complicated, might you be raising another round of money, and why can't you simply take that money from your existing investors?

As we discussed in Chapter 3, the next funding round may have been planned from the outset. Maybe you have a research-heavy business; the first $1 million was intended to take your technology a certain distance – past some important proofs of concept, perhaps – but it was always known at that point that more equity funding would be needed. Or maybe the first $1 million was intended to begin the process of testing the market. If the initial response was positive, and sales showed signs of taking off, the intention was always to raise more money to accelerate that sales growth. Either way, if you are approaching your second round of outside funding having achieved exactly what was planned when you raised your first, congratulations. As you know from Chapter 6, you are part of a small minority.

The majority, though, will be entering their second round of finance against the background of having fallen behind the original plan. Perhaps you are not very far behind, just within the expected tolerances, and you can point to very significant progress since the first round. Perhaps, on the other hand, you are a long way off where you hoped to be. Your development program encountered unexpected complications and overran. Or your first product version was not quite what the market wanted. Or both. Or the investment in sales and marketing did not produce the revenue you hoped. However, now the market opportunity has come into sharper focus. Another investment round will enable you to exploit it. That is the hope, anyway.

INTERNAL ROUNDS

When you raised your first round of funding, you may have assembled a group of investors with pockets deep enough to provide the next injection of finance without recourse to other investors. Although they made no commitment to invest further, as your deal was not "milestone based," the clear intent was to provide further capital if your business was on plan. The added challenge that you took on of a syndicated first round is now looking like a good decision.

Just a moment. Your existing investors are keen to invest further, to "put more money to work," as they say. So that means they think it's a good deal. If it's a good deal for them, is it necessarily a good deal for you? How can you tell whether the terms they are offering are fair? How do you know that there isn't another, stronger investor somewhere out there who will be willing to invest on better terms and leave you with a larger stake in the company?

Obviously, you don't want to go through the pain of bringing in another investor unless you really have to. If you do, you will have to go through the full due diligence process again, and create another full set of legal documents. Any new investor is likely to want to invest in some new instrument, like Series B Preferred Shares, ranking ahead of the first-round Series A investment. If you stick with your existing investors, you should be able to get by with a modest supplementary legal agreement, perhaps a renewal of the warranties, but probably no additional strings.

Also, if your existing backers are keen to invest further, they may view with hostility your desire to test the price they are offering. They are also most likely to be in a position to veto any additional investment. If you are able to secure investment on better terms, your existing investors may use their position to insist on matching those terms. That in itself will make it harder for you to obtain terms from a third party; why should they waste time putting together a deal which an existing shareholder can then snatch away?

So if you possibly can, take your existing investors' money. By all means test out the terms as far as you can. Talk to your *keiretsu* of other CEOs. Make sure that you've kept up to speed with the venture capital trade press. Look at recent follow-on rounds in companies similar to yours. Perhaps you've got to know another Vulture whom you can call to ask for a second opinion on the terms of the deal you're being offered by the incumbents. It's hard for him not to be reasonably honest; after all, if he says that your incumbent investors are offering you a cheap deal, he's coming close to saying that he would be willing to invest at a higher price.

Anyway, by now a relationship of trust and mutual respect should have developed between you and your Angels, Dragons, or Vultures. That trust should tell you that they aren't going to try to rip you off with terms which are predatory; that respect should say that nor are they going to offer you the very best terms available. It may be possible to improve the deal they offer a little, especially if you can find examples of higher-priced follow-on rounds in comparable circumstances. Ultimately, however, just as we agreed in Chapter 4 that it made sense to take your first-round money at a slightly lower price from strong investors with whom you had a rapport, so it is likely to make sense to take follow-on money from your existing investor group if it's on offer on reasonable terms.

Remember that what matters is the ultimate outcome, and don't underestimate the damage and delay that can be caused to your business when you pour the bulk of your energy into raising money from new external investors. By the same token, if your existing investors are experienced, they should be similarly focused on the longer term, and wise enough to offer you terms that are fair and that you will be able to accept without excessive heartache.

BRIDGE ROUNDS

Sometimes it happens that your first round has taken you almost to the point where a good uplift in value could be expected, or at least where a new round can be completed with relative ease. The trouble is, you aren't quite there yet, and the money's about to run out. You're sitting in the board meeting, looking with gloom at the cash flow projections. If only you'd been able to stretch things a bit further.

On the other side of the table, your investor directors turn to each other. With a very serious expression on his face, the first says, "I think maybe we should do the bridge." For an instant you feel shock. It is irritating not to have quite got there, yes, but surely not so desperate that they should be thinking about the long leap from Golden Gate into the water below? Then the penny drops – not the body, thank heavens. They're talking about a "bridge round."

A bridge round is when the existing investors put in enough interim funding to give the company time to raise another full round from at least one new investor. Normally bridge rounds are "unpriced," so that the price paid by the new investor in the next round isn't compromised. The funding is provided in Loan Notes, which then convert to equity when the next round takes place.

That sounds a good deal? Well, basically it is. It demonstrates to the outside world the existing investors' strong support for the business. It gives you a bit more time to take the company past the next valuation milestone. But of course, it doesn't come without some strings attached. Normally bridge Loan Notes will be convertible at a discount to the next round price – perhaps 10%, perhaps 20%, or perhaps a variable discount linked to the length of time for which they're outstanding. Sometimes they also bear interest. They may be secured on the company's assets and intellectual property. But the terms can't be egregious, because if they are, they will put off any new

193

investor, or at least be renegotiated by him as part of the price of his investment.

However, the bridge Loan Notes will normally have back-stop conversion rights. So if the new round hasn't happened within a certain period – say, six or twelve months – they become convertible into equity. The conversion price will probably be that of the last round, because anything different runs the risk of alarming potential incoming investors. But on occasion it might be at a significantly lower price. And in any event, in the absence of a new round, conversion will be at the option of the holder. Thus in practice, if no further round takes place, the investor will continue to hold them as Loan Notes until an exit, perhaps accumulating interest all that time. They will sit on the wrong side of your balance sheet.

If the ultimate exit is a success, your investors will convert at what by then might look a tasty price. If the outcome is a disappointment, your investors will have increased their relative proportion of the proceeds and reduced their downside by staying in Loan Notes. Nevertheless, if your investors are willing to make you a bridge loan, you should view it as a gift horse rather than a Trojan horse and avoid looking it in the mouth.

SERIES B, OR ROUND $N + 1$

There are several reasons your existing investors may expect you to attract a new pugilist to Round 2. Perhaps these were part of the original fund-raising strategy developed in Chapter 3; perhaps circumstances have forced subsequent change.

The first reason is that your existing investors might be thinking that their follow-on reserves may not be enough to see you all the way through to success. Any experienced early-stage investor will reserve at least the amount he invests in the first round for subsequent follow-on, and perhaps twice the initial amount. Even so, you have slipped against your original plan; your Vulture can see the possibility of further slippage and may be getting edgy. Most funds tend to reserve more cash for follow-on investment across their whole portfolio than they have available. They hope that they will not need to use all their reserves, and their caution is tempered by a desire to generate the best possible returns by investing as much of their fund as possible. The usual effect, especially later in the life of a fund, is that reserves become stretched and follow-on money gets scarce.

The second reason is that your Vulture may just be feeling a bit nervous. He may want validation from a third-party investor that your business is still worth backing. Or his personal faith may be unshaken, but he might have been told by his partners that for the firm to "follow their money," external validation is needed. And that is external validation not only of the opportunity, but of the valuation at which it makes sense to invest in that opportunity. Around those investment committee tables on Monday morning there can often be more than a whiff of suspicion that the individual on the case may have "gone native."

The other thought in the minds of those dour-faced individuals around the table (I've never met anyone who admits to enjoying their Monday morning investment meetings) is that companies which require a follow-on round generally deliver poorer returns than those which get by with one round of funding. That certainly applies to businesses which have to raise a second round of funding because they have slipped against plan. Knowing this, they may prefer to limit the amount they invest, aiming to reallocate any reserve they have toward other investment opportunities. They will be balancing that against the risk of sentencing their existing investment to failure, or to a long half-life among the living dead.

Sometimes the Vulture may justify going out to new investors by saying to you that a third-party price is needed to convince you that any proposed deal is fair. Effectively he is

195

expressing the thought that might have passed through your mind about the equitable pricing of the deal if he had proposed an internal round. Or he might cite conflicts of interest: "We have this new fund that we would like to invest, you see. But without a third-party investor to validate the deal and price it, we simply cannot unlock the conflicts of interest."

I touched on these conflicts of interest in Chapter 2. To recap, they arise when a general partner manages more than one fund. Each fund is almost certain to have been raised at least in part from different investors. So some of the limited partners who are only in the new fund will be aligned with brand new investors and want the lowest possible price. Limited partners who are only in the earlier fund want the highest price; those in each fund may have a foot in either camp, depending on the size of their investments. The general partner will therefore be very nervous about the risk of being accused of favoring one group of customers over another, or of having been shown to have done so by subsequent events. Some venture firms have a prohibition on investing in an existing investment from a new fund; others have a mechanism where proposals which give rise to a potential conflict of interest are referred to the Advisory Committee of limited partners for approval. In any case, it makes discussion of these conflicts of interest much more comfortable if a new investor with a completely impartial view is involved.

It may also be that the Vulture wants to have the opportunity to increase the valuation of his investment. His firm is beginning to plan raising its next fund. Normal fund accounting guidelines provide that one of the few circumstances in which an uplift in the valuation of an investment can take place is when another round has taken place at a higher price. Suddenly a short-term valuation increase may be important to him, regardless of the impact over the longer term on the amount of money he ultimately makes on the investment.

RIDING ON YOUR VULTURE'S WINGS

A factor which may mitigate Acland's Law of fund raising is that whereas the first round may have been your first experience of the intricacies of venture capital investment, the second round won't be, by definition; unless, that is, you're a new CEO drafted in since Round 1. Second time around you are likely to understand things better. The second round may be more complex, but most of the same rules apply, like how to prepare your business plan, how to access and approach investors, and the vital need to remain ahead of budget during the fund-raising process. Especially if you used an adviser to help with your first funding round, you may consider whether to use him again.

However, now you should have a significant ally in your Vulture. Your Vulture is already playing a large part in shaping the round. His inability or reluctance to provide all the funding is driving you to go to other investors. Therefore your Vulture should be playing a major part in the process, making sure that you're properly prepared, helping you to identify the right investors to approach, and making useful introductions.

Your objective in the funding round is to raise money at a sensible price from strong investors with a minimum of fuss. Your Vulture will clearly share these objectives. Unless you have lost faith in your Vulture and your relationship with him has deteriorated, you should encourage him to take as leading a role in the fund raising as possible. This is partly because he can shoulder a significant part of the burden and save you a lot of time. But it is also because his active involvement is a good sign to new potential investors and makes success more likely. It shows them that the Vulture really does care about the success of your business, that he is actively engaged, committing his time, and therefore that he expects to make money out of it.

I always used to worry if a business which had already received venture money approached me about its next round via an intermediary. That told me that the company concerned might be a low priority for the investor, or that the relationship had somehow turned sour. Most Vultures know their way around the venture capital market as well as any intermediary and often have an easier entrée to other investors, so it is questionable that involving a corporate finance adviser at this stage will help to raise the money. Lean on your Vulture if he is willing. Think about what conclusions to draw if he is not.

Nevertheless, you do need to be aware that your Vulture may have some other issues at the back of his mind. If he views you as a "hot deal," he will want to introduce you to firms with which he is trying to curry favor. These might include "top-tier" firms in his own region, or in other geographies. The Vulture might be trying to join their club, hoping that if he shows them a good opportunity they will reciprocate. Or they might include the Vulture's own fund investors – his primary customers, after all. It is even possible that he may have an obligation toward some of their limited partners to show them follow-on investment opportunities if possible. That is because some limited partners request co-investment rights when they commit to a fund. Although these co-investment rights are rarely legally binding, there may be a strong moral obligation which the Vulture will be eager to respect in the interests of furthering the relationship with his customer.

He might also want to introduce you to investors who are not yet limited partners in one of his funds, but whom he is wooing.

Unless there is a very powerful reason, in none of these cases should you resist your matchmaker. Indeed, if you can do your Vulture a favor by going to present to a firm on which he wants to make a good impression (and in the course of your presentation, tell them how wonderful the Vulture is), then why not? It can only be a good thing for your relationship and for the future.

There may also be firms with which your Vulture has had a bad experience, where there are partners whom he personally dislikes, or which he views as very direct competitors. He may be reluctant for you to talk to these about the next round. Even if some of them appear to be suitable or even desirable investors to you, you are unlikely to benefit from ignoring your Vulture's preferences. Given the background, this group are anyway unlikely to come up with capital on acceptable terms, if at all. In all probability your own Vulture's feelings toward them will be reciprocated.

If your Vulture is less positive about your progress, he may reach out to a different constituency. He may have friends in his peer group with whom he is comfortable co-investing, who help each other out from time to time. Or he may suggest approaching investors in a lower tier, second- or third-division firms who may be attracted by the opportunity of stepping up a notch and co-investing with his firm. They may see fewer interesting investment opportunities, and may be less discerning. If your Vulture takes this approach, it will at least tell you pretty clearly how he views you and where you stand.

In any event, the best approach is to talk openly and frankly with your Vulture about the strategy for the round. It is much better for both you and him to go into the round with your eyes wide open and with realistic assumptions. Pushing at all costs for an "up round" when you've made little progress since the previous round, or when the world outside has turned much colder, making a "down round" the likelihood, and unrealistically approaching the wrong type of investors as a result, is totally counterproductive.

FOLLOW-ON INVESTMENT

One aspect of the new round that will need to be resolved in advance between you and the Vulture is the amount of money the Vulture will contribute to it. If the original investor is not planning to make any contribution to the new round, alarm bells will ring with the new investor even more loudly than if the Vulture is not helping manage the process. Lack of participation will be viewed as a lack of faith in the company, or in the business plan, or in the entrepreneur. It will open the way for a steep decline in valuation, because although new Vultures may have reservations about diluting management's shareholdings (see later in this chapter), they have no such scruples toward their fellow Vultures. In fact, they secretly love it because they are demonstrating to their own limited partners, their important customers, that they are better at getting a good deal and judging the right time to come in than another general partner (their competitor for the limited partners' money).

The normal default position is that the existing investors contribute their pro rata to the round. This means that if one owns 25% of the equity, that investor will contribute 25% of the money to the new round, to maintain his equity percentage after the round. If he wants to contribute more than 25%, with the result of increasing his percentage stake, it demonstrates not only that he strongly believes in the company's potential, but that he views the price at which the new round is taking place as good value, and likely to enhance his return in IRR terms. If he drops a long way below his pro rata, it may begin to look as if he thinks that the round is quite expensive, even if his faith in the company's potential is unshaken. Of course, if the incoming investor is pushing to invest a larger amount than can be accommodated, the existing investor can gracefully make way and do less than his pro rata without much risk of damage.

Once there are two or more Vultures in an investment, the rules of engagement change somewhat. I deal with these dynamics a little later in the chapter.

UP, DOWN, SHAKE IT ALL AROUND

I apologize for having lapsed into jargon without explaining it first, although in this case you hardly deserve a prize for working out the difference between an up round and a down round. An up round is what everyone wants, when the pre-money valuation of your company in the new round exceeds the post-money valuation of the previous round. On a fully diluted basis, naturally. It is most simply defined by saying that the price per share goes up from one round to the next.

A down round is the opposite. It can be caused by internal or external circumstances. The internal circumstance which usually causes a down round is when progress in the company has been disappointing but not calamitous (because then there would probably be no round at all). One way of looking at it is that the proceeds of the previous round have not been spent so as to increase the value of the business by as much as the cash invested. So the pre-money valuation of the new round is lower than the post-money of the old round, and the share price goes down. Note that it is possible to have a down round where the post-money of the new round is higher than the post-money of the old round, but where the difference is not as great as the money invested in the old round. So the headline post-money valuation may nudge forward, but the price per share still goes down.

The external circumstance prompting a down round is when the investment climate has worsened. A sector has fallen out of favor, and quoted share prices have dropped, or there is just a shortage of capital for investment in venture capital deals and demand exceeds supply, in this case forcing the price down. A very common cause of the many down rounds in the early 2000s, in the aftermath of the burst technology bubble, was simply that many investments had been made at completely unjustifiably elevated valuations.

An up round takes place in an atmosphere of triumphant serenity. Dilution is of course taking place, but it is reduced because the valuation of the company is marching forward. The new money will normally be invested in an instrument which ranks ahead of the previous round. Typically the investment will be made in Series B Preference Shares, or Series C Preferred Stock, or whichever letter's appropriate. Typically these second-, third-, and nth-round instruments will enjoy liquidation preference rights over everything that has gone before. So the valuation tricks of the trade that we discussed in Chapter 4 all apply.

Let's return to the simple example we used in that chapter. $1 million was invested in our company in Series A Preferred Shares for 25% of the equity. There were 3 million shares of common stock (or Ordinary Shares) in issue before the round, so 1 million new Series A Preferred Shares were issued at $1 each. These are participating shares, so they are entitled to the amount paid for them first, and then their equity percentage of 25%. So although the "headline" post-money valuation was $4 million (the amount invested of $1 million divided by the equity percentage of 25%, or the 4 million shares in issue multiplied by the $1 share price), the $1 million liquidation preference needs to be taken into account as well.

If we say that the Series B round involves an investment of $2 million at twice the price, then 1 million Series B Preferred Shares are issued at $2 each. We are now beginning to have a more complex "capitalization table" ("cap table" for short) which looks like this:

	Ordinary Shares	Series A Preferred Shares	Series B Preferred Shares	Total	Equity %
Management	3,000,000			3,000,000	60%
First investor		1,000,000		1,000,000	20%
Second investor			1,000,000	1,000,000	20%
Total				5,000,000	100%

The headline valuation based on the $2 price per share is now $10 million. The first investor still owns 1 million shares, notionally worth $2 million at this price. He now has 20% of the equity, having been diluted by 20% from 25%. The valuation based on share price tallies with his 20% equity stake, being worth $2 million ($10 million × 20%). So the first investor could argue for the revaluation of his original investment of $1 million at $2 million, and he is beginning to look like a hero. Except, of course, that ignores the effect of the two liquidation preferences, now totaling $3 million. If the company were sold at the $10 million headline price, his investment would really be worth $2.4 million (($10 million − $3 million) × 20% + $1 million). And the new Series B investor, at an exit price of $10 million, would actually get $3.4 million − his $2 million liquidation preference plus his 20% share of the remaining $7 million after the $3 million liquidation preference has been paid out. So he invests at a $10 million valuation, and he has already made 1.7 times his money at that exit valuation! The ordinary shareholders, of course, are the ones who suffer, taking away $4.2 million at the $10 million exit in spite of having a 60% equity stake.

These complexities are shown in the table overleaf. (Note that the proceeds formula does not work until the total proceeds exceed the preferences.)

Now let's just suppose that the Series A Vulture obtains two offers from his Series B friends. The first is as just described. The second sounds even better: it is at a share price of $3. That implies only issuing 666,667 Series B Preferred Shares, and means that dilution is reduced to 14.29%. It should also mean that the first Vulture can push the case for revaluing his investment to $3 million, looking an even bigger hero than before, and accelerating his firm's fund-raising progress. The new cap table is shown on page 205.

ANGELS, DRAGONS AND VULTURES

Distribution of proceeds after Series B round – Example 1

Exit price	A	At invest-ment	$2,000,000	$3,000,000	$5,000,000	$10,000,000	$20,000,000	Formula
Investor 1								
Amount invested	B	$1,000,000	$1,000,000	$1,000,000	$1,000,000	$1,000,000	$1,000,000	
Investor 1 proceeds	C		$0	$1,000,000	$1,400,000	$2,400,000	$4,400,000	B + ((A– B–G) x 20%)
Investor 1 share	D	20%	0%	33%	28%	24%	22%	C/A
Effective post-money valuation	E	$5,000,000	$0	$3,000,000	$3,570,000	$4,167,000	$5,880,000	B/D
Effective pre-money valuation	F	$3,000,000	$0	$1,000,000	$1,570,000	$2,167,000	$3,880,000	(B/D) – G
Investor 2								
Amount invested	G	$2,000,000	$2,000,000	$2,000,000	$2,000,000	$2,000,000	$2,000,000	
Investor 2 proceeds	H		$2,000,000	$2,000,000	$2,400,000	$3,400,000	$5,400,000	G + ((A– B–G) x 20%)
Investor 2 share	I	20%	100%	67%	48%	34%	27%	H/A
Effective post-money valuation	J	$10,000,000	$2,000,000	$3,000,000	$4,167,000	$4,545,000	$9,090,000	I/G
Effective pre-money valuation	K	$8,000,000	$0	$1,000,000	$2,167,000	$2,545,000	$7,090,000	(I/G) – G
Managem't								
Managem't proceeds	L		$0	$0	$1,200,000	$4,200,000	$10,200,000	A – C – H
Managem't %	M	60%	0%	0%	24%	42%	51%	100% – D – I

204

	Ordinary Shares	Series A Preferred Shares	Series B Preferred Shares	Total	Equity %
Management	3,000,000			3,000,000	64.3%
First investor		1,000,000		1,000,000	21.4%
Second investor			666,667	666,667	14.3%
Total				4,666,667	100%

However, there is a catch. This Series B instrument has a 2× liquidation preference, so $4 million has to be paid back before the rest of the shareholders get anything. Now, at a $10 million exit, the Series A investor only gets back just over $2 million, in spite of having a headline valuation on a per share basis of $3 million. The table overleaf shows the impact on the Ordinary and Series A Shareholders. (Note again that the proceeds formula does not work until the total proceeds exceed the preferences.)

It is only when the company's value exceeds $33 million (the point at which the difference in the new investor's equity percentage of 5.7% equals the value of the $2 million additional preference) that this deal is better for Investor 1 and the management team. If you, and your first investor, really do believe that this level of exit is realistic, perhaps this is the option you should go for.

But one hopes that the temptation of revaluing his original investment threefold from cost (if his auditors overlook the impact of the liquidation preference, that is, as they often do) does not push the Vulture toward this second option.

In practice, for the sake of clarity, I have somewhat over-simplified the picture, because normally the first investor will be participating alongside the second investor and taking a piece of the Series B round himself.

ANGELS, DRAGONS AND VULTURES

Distribution of proceeds after Series B round – Example 2

Exit price	A	At invest-ment	$2,000,000	$3,000,000	$5,000,000	$10,000,000	$20,000,000	Formula
Investor 1								
Amount invested	B	$1,000,000	$1,000,000	$1,000,000	$1,000,000	$1,000,000	$1,000,000	
Investor 1 proceeds	C		$0	$0	$1,000,000	$2,070,000	$4,210,000	B + ((A–B–G) x 21.4%)
Investor 1 share	D	21.4%	0%	0%	20%	20.7%	21.1%	C/A
Effective post-money valuation	E	$5,000,000	$0	$0	$5,000,000	$4,831,000	$4,739,000	B/D
Effective pre-money valuation	F	$3,000,000	$0	$0	$3,000,000	$2,831,000	$2,739,000	(B/D) – G
Investor 2								
Amount invested	G	$2,000,000	$2,000,000	$2,000,000	$2,000,000	$2,000,000	$2,000,000	
Investor 2 proceeds	H		$2,000,000	$3,000,000	$4,000,000	$4,715,000	$6,145,000	G + ((A–B–G) x 14.3%)
Investor 2 share	I	14.3%	100%	100%	80%	47.2%	30.7%	H/A
Effective post-money valuation	J	$10,000,000	$2,000,000	$3,000,000	$5,000,000	$10,000,000	$9,090,000	I/G
Effective pre-money valuation	K	$8,000,000	$0	$1,000,000	$3,000,000	$8,000,000	$7,090,000	(I/G) – G
Managem't								
Managem't proceeds	L		$0	$0	$0	$3,215,000	$9,645,000	A – C – H
Managem't %	M	64.3%	0%	0%	0%	32.1%	48.2%	100% – D – I

DOWN ROUNDS

If, in spite of those tricky calculations, that up round took place in a mood of triumphant serenity, just imagine the mood when a down round has to occur. A Stygian gloom descends, and in the murk a battle takes place between the shareholders who are the unfortunate denizens of the down round hell.

Why so? you might ask. Surely everyone suffers some painful dilution, and the Vulture may face the humiliation of having to devalue his investment, but at least everyone's in Charon's boat together.

Not necessarily so. Follow one path through the numbers in our example. Let's say that the best offer from a new investor is to invest $2 million for 40% of the equity, giving a post-money headline valuation of $5 million. Let's say that the Series A investor neglected to insist on anti-dilution warrants and feels a bit sore about this.

The ordinary shareholders – you the entrepreneur and perhaps other founding shareholders – might expect to dilute by 40%. That would take you from 75% to 45%. You might also expect the stake of the Series A Preference Shareholder – the Vulture – to decline by the same 40%, so declining from 25% to 15%. The Vulture may have other ideas. "What about my preference?" he may argue. "Pre-money this deal values the company at $3 million. That means that I own 50% of the pre-money: my $1 million preference, plus my equity percentage – 25% – of the remaining $2 million. That makes $1.5 million in total – 50%. So after the Series B round the new investor has 40%, you have 30%, and I have 30%."

You answer that his argument has no validity, that the liquidation preference is intended to provide some downside protection when the value of the company is finally crystallized on exit, and that he will retain the liquidation preference after the Series B round; behind the new investor, of course. You will probably win the argument. But it is harder to hold your position if, say, his original investment was partly in Loan Stock and had rights to accumulate interest, or had cumulative dividend rights, and he is being asked to waive or reduce these rights as a condition of the incoming investment.

If he did have anti-dilution warrants, you have little room for maneuver. By the rules of the game, as explained in Chapter 4, if the investor insisted on full ratchet anti-dilution, he will suffer no dilution in his position at all, and after the round will still own 25%, with the new investor at 40%. You ordinary shareholders will take all the pain and suffer the reduction in your equity from 75% to 35%. If weighted average anti-dilution is the name of the game, you aren't suffering quite as much, but you're still taking a pasting.

Imagine now that your down round comes in Round 3. You have your original Series A investor. Things were going well a year in: you hadn't made many sales but not many had been planned; the product was fully developed and looked as if it was beginning to get "market traction." So you were able to raise the second round, the B round, at a mark-up to the first round. Let's assume that a new investment of $2 million was raised at a price of $2 per share. Let's also assume for reality's sake that the original investor contributed his pro rata of the second round: $500,000 of the $2 million total in view of his 25% stake.

Before the round everything is rosy and the cap table looks like this:

	Ordinary Shares	Series A Preferred Shares	Series B Preferred Shares	Total	Equity %
Management	3,000,000			3,000,000	60%
First investor		1,000,000	250,000	1,250,000	25%
Second investor			750,000	750,000	15%
Total	3,000,000	1,000,000	1,000,000	5,000,000	100%

Unfortunately, though, the market traction hasn't translated into sales as quickly as hoped. Some early adopters have bought the product, but, surprise, surprise, it has taken longer than anticipated to cross the chasm and enter the mainstream. Another round is going to be needed, and to really put some rocket fuel in the tank $5 million is required. That's too much for the two existing investors to provide. They expect the new Vulture to bring $3 million to the table, which would leave $2 million to be found by the existing investors.

Pro rata to their equity percentages, the first and second investors should invest $1.25 million and $750,000 respectively. But in fact, the first investor is hoping to avoid having to invest his full pro rata. As a first-round-focused investor, his funds are smaller than the second investor's, and much smaller than the third investor's, who has a later-stage focus. Even if he could scrape together $1.25 million, he would then be very exposed if there needed to be another round, because he would have nothing left to contribute to it. The third investor might even impose terms which would wash the first out completely. So the first investor would like the second investor to agree to go pro rata to the amounts each of them has invested, which would mean $1 million each. Or even better, to agree to go pro rata to the amounts they contributed to the Series B round, which would be a $500,000 : $1.5 million split.

Meanwhile, the second investor is feeling sore. His entry capitalization is $10 million. Even though the first investor contributed pro rata to that round, because of the big increase in price he is in at an average capitalization of only $6 million. The second investor knows that one of his own limited partners is also an investor in the first investor's fund. He therefore runs the risk of being made to look a fool in front of one of his key customers.

Suddenly the picture's looking rather messy. The Vultures' interests are diverging, and dangerous rivalries are appearing. If the first investor says too soon that he does not want to invest his share of the round, the second investor might work out that it is in his own longer-term interests actually to push the share price of the new round down. Or the second investor might try to fight his corner by arguing the case for the preference on the Series B Preference Shares, which after all do rank ahead of the first-round instrument. However, if the third investor detects tensions between the existing investor group, he might be able to exploit them in his turn, or the tensions might put him off making the investment at all.

FLAT ROUNDS

A flat round is not an argument between two medieval philosophers about the shape of the world, nor even the contradiction in terms it appears to be. It simply means another round of funding taking place at the same share price as the last round. Because Vultures dislike owning up to down rounds so much, they sometimes describe rounds at the same headline valuation as before as "flat," but in reality there's no getting away from it: if the share price has gone down, it's a down round.

MANAGEMENT LEVERAGE AND THE "STACK"

I can imagine that while you've been reading the section above about the unpleasant consequences of down rounds, one thought has been at the forefront of your mind: "What happens to me in all of this?" If Vultures are trying to crush each other, surely the management team, without significant money to invest, will be torn to bloody pieces between them.

Actually, the management team has more leverage than you might think. This is because new Vultures will only invest in a company if they believe that the management team is relatively content and well motivated. They may relish diluting the early-round investors out of sight and enjoy demonstrating how much smarter than their competitors they are. Nevertheless, they will want to make sure that the management team is fairly treated, and that there are enough spare options in the pool to attract and retain future members of the team. To an extent this applies to an internal round as well: your existing investors should not want the management team to be excessively diluted, which is good news; provided, of course, that you are part of it going forward. If you're considered to be part of the reason for the plan going off track, and for the new dilutive round taking place, you may find yourself focusing on the good leaver/bad leaver clauses in the legal documentation rather than calculating by how much your options need to be refreshed.

There are really two main areas that may trouble an incoming investor. One, as I have implied, are the options. In the examples I used in the previous section about down rounds, I left out options because of the additional complications they introduce. But let's now put them into the latest example, so that the cap table is on a fully diluted basis (once all the available options have been granted and exercised). Let's say that there's a 15% option pool. In a company still at a relatively early stage, investors would begin to get concerned if it fell much below that level.

	Ordinary Shares	Series A Preferred Shares	Series B Preferred Shares	Total	Equity %
Management	3,000,000			3,000,000	51%
First investor		1,000,000	250,000	1,250,000	21.25%
Second investor			750,000	750,000	12.75%
Options	882,353			882,353	15%
Total	3,882,353	1,000,000	1,000,000	5,882,353	100%

As one would expect, the effect of including the options in the table is simply to reduce all the shareholders' equity percentages by 15%. Another way of looking at it is that all shareholders' entry capitalizations have increased by 15%, so the second investor, who has paid $2 for all his shares, has a post-money fully diluted entry capitalization of $11.76 million, up from $10 million before options; and the first investor, who has paid $1 for his Series A Prefs and $2 for his Series Bs, now has an entry capitalization of $7.06 million, up from $6 million before options. Incidentally, while it is not wholly logical, the exercise price of the options is normally ignored in these discussions.

Now, smiles all round because a new investor has been identified who will invest $3 million in Series C Preference Shares, alongside a further $1 million from each of the existing investors, who have shelved their differences and agreed to go 50/50. The new investor has agreed to invest at a price of $1 per share, or a fully diluted post-money valuation of $10,882,353. Now the cap table looks like this:

	Ordinary Shares	Series A Preferred Shares	Series B Preferred Shares	Series C Preferred Shares	Total	Equity %
Management	3,000,000				3,000,000	27.57%
First investor		1,000,000	250,000	1,000,000	2,250,000	20.68%
Second investor			750,000	1,000,000	1,750,000	16.08%
Third investor				3,000,000	3,000,000	27.57%
Options	882,353				882,353	8.11%
Total	3,882,353	1,000,000	1,000,000	5,000,000	10,882,353	100%

So has the down round gloom turned into sweetness and light? Unfortunately, not yet. The first and second investors are somewhat relieved to have a deal at all. But now the management team are up in arms. Not only has their real equity stake been pasted from 51% to 28%, but the available option pool has gone to 8% from 15%. Recruitment to several key positions is planned to drive the next phase of growth, and that is not going to be enough to attract them, especially as one of the founders will have to be granted some options in order to counterbalance some of his equity dilution.

So now the third investor gets worried: "We're not going to have enough options to recruit good people going forward. And there are probably some key people in the existing team who need an option refresh." The first and second investors exchange glances, wondering whether the third investor spotted this issue for himself, or whether he's been got at by the management team. "We need to top the pool back up to 15%."

No problem so far, one might think. Just double the number of options in the pool to get back to 15%. "Uh-uh, no way," says the third Vulture. "I said I would invest at a fully diluted post-money of $10,882,353. You are asking me to take that up to $11,764,706. No can do. The existing shareholders will have to refresh the pool before the new-round investment takes place."

After a lot of squawking, the first two Vultures have to agree to a cap table that looks like the one overleaf.

The effect, of course, is to drive the price per Series C Preferred Share to $0.85, because the new subscribers need more shares for their $5 million in order to maintain their own position in the face of a 15% option pool. A side effect is to dilute the management equity (likely to be held by the founders and early employees) still further, from 27.57% to 23.43%. Although this is more than balanced by the increase in the option pool from 8.11% to 15%, it probably signposts a shift in equity ownership from the early members of the team

	Ordinary Shares	Series A Preferred Shares	Series B Preferred Shares	Series C Preferred Shares	Total	Equity %
Management	3,000,000				3,000,000	23.43%
First investor		1,000,000	250,000	1,176,593	2,426,593	18.95%
Second investor			750,000	1,176,593	1,926,593	15.05%
Third investor				3,529,778	3,529,778	27.57%
Options	1,920,615				1,920,615	15%
Total	4,920,615	1,000,000	1,000,000	5,882,964	12,804,099	100%

toward newer recruits brought in, or to be brought in, to take the company on to the next level.

However, that may not be all. "I'm worried about the effect of the stack on the team," says the third Vulture.

By this he does not mean chimney stack, of course, but the preference stack – the amount that has to be paid to the preferred shareholders before the ordinary shareholders, in other words the management, receive a cent.

"Obviously the new Series C Stock will have to keep its preference, but if we eliminate the preferred rights from the Series A and Series B then we reduce the stack by $3 million, so that the team are in the money above $5 million."

The first and second Vultures look at each other again, wondering again just what has been said by the management team to the third Vulture. From the steely glint in that Vulture's eye they ascertain that this is a deal breaker and are forced to accept the elimination of their earlier preferences in order to get the round away.

So follow-on funding rounds, especially of the "down" variety, will be painful for the entrepreneur and his team, but sometimes perhaps less painful than one might think, because of the overriding concern of the incoming investor that the team should be motivated and incentivized.

However, as with other remuneration issues, pushing your own position too hard is likely to be counterproductive (see Chapter 9). The conversation that you may or may not have had with the newest Vulture needs to be carefully judged. If your investors are paying a financial penalty, either by suffering dilution or reducing their returns as a result of investing more, it is only reasonable that you should suffer a little too. If you don't accept that, the ultimate outcome may be more painful.

And as with all remuneration issues, if you have a strong chairman who is able to intercede on your behalf where necessary and take the sting out of difficult conversations, so much the better.

TRADE INVESTORS

Sometimes, when the investor group is contemplating the need for another funding round and whom to approach, one of the Vultures' faces will light up and they will say: "What about a trade investor?"

There may be a number of motives behind this comment. First, the Vulture may have heard a lot of talk at previous board meetings about how well the relationship with A Corp is progressing. You might have talked about signing a partnership agreement, or the way in which they are beginning to open doors into new customers. The Vulture is likely to have heard a lot of this before, and may be rather cynical about it, because often these "special" relationships do not bear significant commercial fruit. So the suggestion that A Corp might like to contribute to the round may be partly motivated by a desire to test the strength of the relationship. And if an industry partner does agree to invest, it does indeed provide a strong endorsement.

Secondly, as well as giving a good signal to your existing Vultures, a trade investor is likely to encourage other new financial investors. Even if most large corporations are inexperienced as venture capital investors, they probably know more about their market than most Vultures.

Thirdly, the involvement of a trade investor may bring commercial benefits. Clearly, it may be possible to sign a distribution agreement, or a research collaboration, without equity investment alongside. But having the trade partner as an equity investor too will, the theory goes, motivate them to make the relationship work because they will be able to see the equity upside.

Finally, that spark deep at the back of your Vulture's eyes may be partly attributable to the thought that the trade investor may provide the perfect exit opportunity.

So are trade investors a thoroughly good thing? Do you follow up your Vulture's suggestion as vigorously as you know how? Well, perhaps, but bear in mind the following.

First, very few large corporations regularly make investments in small partners. Venture investing, with one or two exceptions, is just not part of their business. At the time of the technology boom many corporations did set up venture capital arms, but few of these prospered or survived when the downturn came. The enterprises which regularly do venture investing tend to organize this activity in a separate division. This means that they behave in a similar way to a Vulture: there may be some relationship benefits with the trading arms of the enterprise, but a trade investment does not necessarily guarantee that your product will begin to fly off their shelves or through their distribution pipeline.

Secondly, how do you approach your trade partner about investment without risking the relationship? The individuals you are dealing with commercially are highly unlikely of themselves to be able to sanction an equity investment. The finance department, possibly right up to the CFO himself, will almost certainly have to be involved in the decision-making process. Some awkward questions may also emerge. "Why are we building a strategic relationship with a small company which needs more equity investment to survive?" may be one. Obviously, before the investment takes place, they will want to look at your accounts just like any other investor. All the effort you have made to appear to them like a $10 million revenue business instead of a $5 million business may be destroyed.

Thirdly, you may be entering a corporate political minefield. Your product may be challenging one of your trade partner's existing products, or an internal product development program. So far you may have avoided getting too much in the face of the internal champions of the alternative approach. Raising your profile with an equity investment proposal may turn you into the focus for hostile fire.

Finally, maybe you do not enhance your exit prospects. Maybe, by making one large corporation a shareholder, you will simply put off their competitors from collaborating with you or trying to buy you in the future. Maybe your new investor can get everything they need from you for a minority stake, so that they never have to buy the rest of the equity. Or maybe, because such a high proportion of your revenue becomes dependent on them, they can force a takeover at a knock-down price.

Having said all that, a trade investor can be beneficial provided that you stick to certain rules:

❑ Do not allow a trade investor to buy a stake which will give them excess influence; think very hard indeed before you allow them to go over 10%.

❑ Make sure that they do not have veto rights over decisions that they might want to block for narrow reasons of their own – such as a sale of the business.

❑ In no circumstances give them the right of first refusal to buy the business, or to match another bid; this simply means that nobody else will bother to make an offer.

❏ Do not allow a trade investment to become a condition of a round proceeding either for your existing investors or new investors; it is an outside chance

❏ Do not approach your potential trade investor until the terms of the round are agreed and the other investors lined up. You need to be able to go to them in certainty that your funding is there, so that they do not start to worry about your financial viability, and they are unlikely to have the skills to determine what is and is not a good price, so you have to offer them the deal on a plate.

HOW DO YOU HANDLE A WHOLE NEST OF VULTURES?

In Chapter 3 I touched on the pros and cons of raising the first round of money from one investor, or from a group of investors. Whatever your decision then, you are likely to have more than one investor after your second round. So this is where I am going to cover how best to handle a syndicate of investors.

One of the first things that you will have to accept is that you will have a series of relationships to manage. It is definitely not enough to cultivate just your lead investor, if you have one. You may have one investor who is larger and more active than the others and describes himself as the "lead." (Or, Vultures being Vultures, you may have more than one who describes himself as the lead.) The lead investor may do some of the work of corralling the rest of the investor group, but you will have to do most of the communication yourself.

You will also have to accept that your board is likely to become bigger than you ideally want. Each investor will probably want a presence at the table. Some of your smaller investors may be content with "observer rights," where they can send a representative to the board meeting to listen, speak, but not vote. Others will want the formal right to appoint a director; in some cases, if you have one especially large investor, he may even want the right to appoint two. Normally the nominated directors will be employees of the venture firm itself, and probably the individual with whom you did the deal. But sometimes you will come across investors who have the policy of appointing non-employees, perhaps older individuals with more experience, possibly specifically in your industry sector. That can be helpful, although you may well then find yourself with an observer from those firms too. If not, you will have a longer communication chain to manage, and you will need to check from time to time that the outside director is reporting effectively back to the people who appointed him.

Before you know it you will be well past the point of having an ideal four or five directors around the table. With observers and all, you may soon find that your conference room is cramped with nine or ten. I'm afraid that you are well on the way to having a Vulture-dominated board, which may suffer from the drawbacks I described at the end of Chapter 7. Nevertheless, do not succumb to the temptation, also described in that chapter, of moving your meetings to the large boardroom at their place.

Remember what I have said several times earlier in this book about the benefits of having a good chairman? Perhaps earlier on you worried about the dilution of your authority. It may fill another seat around the table. But if you were not persuaded before, I hope that the prospect of handling a whole nest of Vultures will convince you. You will need the chairman to help with the communication, the organization, and occasionally to whip unruly Vulture directors into line. But above all, you need him to act as a lightning conductor.

Your investors will all talk to each other before and after board meetings (and during them too, for that matter). Your ears will be permanently burning. Sometimes the investors will agree with each other. Sometimes there may be disagreements, or differences of emphasis. Quite often the early-stage investors – probably those who joined you in the first or Series A round – will have a more relaxed view of risk, and be more accustomed to slippage against budget. Later-stage investors may be used to bigger, more established businesses, and may be spooked more easily if things go off track. They may also expect more formal processes and organization.

These issues are much more easily handled by a chairman than by the CEO. The chairman should be talking to all the investors before the meeting, identifying issues of concern and areas of potential conflict. They should then discuss the issues with you. Some may be valid; some may be caused by poor communication and thus also valid, or may be at least partially of your own making; others may have no substance at all. Your chairman should develop a plan with you for resolving these issues in the board meeting and for reaching the best decisions for the business. Then, after the meeting, he should be back in contact with the board members and observers again to make sure that they are content. If issues are not tackled they will typically become more extreme and may ultimately explode, taking you with them.

CHAPTER TWELVE

Exits

The end of the long winding road?

Your ultimate aim when seeking investment may be eventually to exit the business by a successful sale that makes you a significant pile of money. In other circumstances, unfortunately, the choice may not be yours – and that is where we begin this chapter.

INVOLUNTARY EXITS

Involuntary exits – insolvencies – are an unavoidable fact of venture capital life. In fact, some say that you cannot become a rounded venture capital investor until you have been on the board of at least one company that has failed. Some also say that the same applies to becoming a proper entrepreneur. I don't go quite as far as that, since avoiding failure is best of all. But I do agree that you cannot claim your spurs as either venture capitalist or entrepreneur unless you have at least glanced over the edge of the precipice and gazed down into the abyss.

The complex subject of insolvency is beyond the scope of this book. Laws and regulations vary from territory to territory, and they change regularly. So I'm not going to try to cover them here, I'm merely going to make two observations.

The first is simple. If you are close to the edge of the precipice – if you are technically insolvent, meaning that your liabilities exceed your assets, and if there is a risk that you may not be able to meet your liabilities as and when they fall due – take formal advice from a good insolvency practitioner, be certain that you understand that advice, and make sure that you follow it carefully.

I make the second point because this is a book about the relationship between entrepreneur and investor. From time to time, when a company has got into a tight corner, I have seen investor directors become excessively cautious. Safeguarding their personal reputations can become more important to them than the interests of the creditors of the business of which they are a director. Many of the businesses in which I have been involved have become technically insolvent, with their liabilities exceeding their assets for a period of time, but have quite properly and correctly continued to trade. The board has looked carefully at the cash flow projections and made the judgment, based on reasonable assumptions, that there is a realistic prospect of the company being able to meet its obligations as and when they fall due. Perhaps that judgment has been based on the expectation of completing a successful fund -raising, or closing an important sale.

The majority of those companies have gone on to succeed: the cash did come in, the creditors were paid, the business flourished, the employees kept their jobs, and the shareholders made money. Rash exuberance can lead to improper behavior and a failure to guard the interests of those toward whom directors have a responsibility – but so can excessive caution.

MANAGEMENT BUY-BACKS

Right back in Chapter 1, I said that by taking outside investment you were setting off on a path which led to selling or floating your business, and that the chances of buying it back again if you changed your mind were small. In most instances, I said, that opportunity would only emerge if things had gone disappointingly badly.

Sometimes this does happen through insolvency, and the management team can buy part or all of the broken business from the administrator or receiver. On occasions this may be fair enough. Perhaps you really did try your best to make the company succeed in its previous incarnation. Perhaps there was some fatal flaw in the business model or structure which the insolvency process has been able to eliminate. Or perhaps your existing backer was unwilling to fund you further or to allow new funding to take place on feasible terms. Nevertheless, you were able to find a new investor to support you in buying the business from the receiver. This might provide the best solution in the circumstances for your original company's creditors (including, of course, the employees). If the motivation was fair, and everything was legal and above board, well, better luck next time. If not, I hope you will struggle to look at yourself in the mirror in the morning.

Sometimes a business can simply plod along. It survives, but never flourishes. The external investment has not provided the desired impetus: the product development failed, say, and the business had to fall back on the consultancy activities with which it started. There is no realistic prospect of selling it, let alone achieving an IPO; it needs to go back to being a "lifestyle business" generating a living for the participants, but not creating any capital value. Nevertheless, your Vulture needs to get out: his 10-year fund is near its end and he has to give back to his customers whatever value he can salvage. Or perhaps your Angel has lost patience and wants to go back to golf.

A buy-back may be the only solution. These deals can be very painful to negotiate. On the one hand, you want to obtain the best deal you can in order to free the company from the shackles of its external shareholder and to return it to your ownership; on the other hand, that external shareholder wants to recoup as much of his investment as possible. Indeed, if you have a Vulture, it is his fiduciary responsibility to do so;

if you have an Angel or a Dragon his position will be more personal.

Either way, the morning mirror should be a good test of where to draw the line. If you believe with honest justification that your investor has done his best to take advantage of you along the way, has been obstructive, perhaps has even contributed to the dire straits your company has reached, well, you may be justified in driving as hard a bargain as you can and leveraging your position of strength as the leader of the management team. However, if your investor has been a reasonable partner, if he has done what he could to help the business, remember that you are the one who has failed to fulfill your part of the bargain. Bear that in mind when you are discussing the buy-back price. Remember too that your investor is likely to have enough rights under the Shareholders' Agreement to make your life pretty uncomfortable if he believes you are trying to take unfair advantage of him. Think about your personal reputation. The world of Angels, Dragons, and Vultures is quite small. If you do rip off your equity backer, you are likely to be saying goodbye to the chance of raising external investment for a business of yours in the future, because your actions will show up in the next due diligence process.

TRADE SALE OR IPO?

Now let's look on the bright side. Let's assume that you, and your investors, have achieved what you all set out to do. You have built a flourishing, valuable business and want to cash in your chips. Actually, of course, if you want to cash them in right now you've left it too late, because you should have started thinking about your exit well before you wanted to achieve it. You cannot just walk straight out of this casino.

Personally, I have never believed that it's possible to plan an exit with precision a long way in advance. There are too many unknowns; too much is outside your control. It is just not possible to say: "We will build this business for four years and then do an initial public offering on Nasdaq." Stock markets open and close. Different types of business come in and out of favor; different sectors fade in and out of fashion. You may be smart enough to predict some of those trends, but you will need extraordinarily good luck to get them absolutely right.

Nor is it realistic to say: "In three years' time we will sell out to Microsoft." Large corporations change direction and management, and even get bought themselves. Nevertheless, some elements are under your control. You can get these right and groom your company with the objective of having an IPO or stock exchange flotation as an option. And it is possible to adapt your strategy to make an acquisition by a particular enterprise more likely – or less likely if you aren't careful.

None of that should be allowed to get in the way of the task of building a good business, however, because that achievement in itself is what will keep most options open and make ultimate success in one of them most likely. It will also give you the option of continuing to run the business and of picking your own time for the exit.

A good starting point is to understand the differences between an exit via trade sale and an exit via IPO. Actually, I'm sorry, I got that sentence wrong. Let me start again. The sentence should read: "A good starting point is to understand the differences between a trade sale and an IPO." Because for you, neither of them is an immediate exit. For your Angel, Dragon, or Vulture the former may be an exit, and the latter may lead that way relatively quickly. *You* will have to be far more patient.

TRADE SALE

A trade sale brings you closer to an exit than an IPO, so let's start with that first. And you may still be worrying about why a trade sale is not an immediate exit for you, so let's put you out of your misery.

In a trade sale, another business, typically a larger one, buys yours. You receive an amount of cash which you put into your bank account. Surely that's an exit? To the extent that you have received money, yes it is. But you are likely to have an obligation to continue working in the business for a certain period, maybe a year, maybe two, perhaps even longer. You may be due future payments linked to your continued employment. All or some of that may also depend on the performance of the business going forward.

When you sell the business you will be required to give the purchaser warranties, similar in style to the warranties you gave your Vulture or Angel when you raised capital. They are similar in style but different in effect, because whereas investment warranties are rarely invoked, acquisition warranties sometimes are. Possibly some of the consideration you have been paid can be clawed back if the sold assets turn out to be worth less than expected, if a debtor is not collectible, or if an outstanding lawsuit goes the wrong way. More likely, any shortfall will be deducted from an escrow account in which part of the consideration due to you is lodged, or set against deferred consideration that is due to be paid at a later date. But probably the escrow account and the deferred consideration will not cover your maximum liability under the warranties. So you have the money in your bank account, yes, but there's an admittedly small but definite chance that you might be sued for some of it down the line. Most of the warranties will most probably last until two new sets of audited accounts have been prepared, so for more than one year but less than two. Some warranties, relating to tax for example, may last for six years.

Some of your consideration may have been paid in equity in the acquiring company. They want you to stay with them, running your business under their corporate umbrella. That is flattering, in a way. So they offer you a good chunk of options as part of the deal which vest over a three-year period. If you have received shares in the acquirer instead of cash as part or all of the consideration they will most likely be restricted, meaning that you cannot sell them for a particular period, and then only through the acquirer's bankers or stockbrokers. Maybe their stock goes up, so you end up getting a better deal. However, it might equally go down, and the money that was going to fund your next business, or enable you never to work again, may steadily trickle away.

So how should you look at all this? The first thing to be very clear about is that from a money point of view an exit is not an exit until it is in cash in your bank account. You should look at your deferred consideration, especially if it is performance linked or tied to conditions such as escrow, as a bonus when it arrives. If some of your payment is in shares, you should only count on that when the shares are sold and the proceeds banked.

As for your commitment to remain employed, you should be prepared for the worst. Sometimes, everything works out well post-acquisition. The wooing that has taken place during the acquisition process starts a genuine love affair. The cultural fit is good: the greater breadth and larger resources of the buyer mean that you can now complete those product developments and tackle those markets of which you could only dream when you were independent. Refreshing challenges and opportunities open up in the new corporate environment for you and your team.

Unfortunately, it is more common that disenchantment sets in. The entrepreneurial spark that characterized your company before it was bought is more often snuffed out by the new owners. They don't mean to do so; indeed, they would dearly love to keep it going. But you are faced with the larger enterprise's reporting lines, their control requirements, the intricacies of their budgeting, and their public company pressures. It all conspires to deaden your lively working environment. If you have been bought by an overseas corporation there will be myriad tiresome little cultural differences to contend with as well, mis- understandings of style and vocabulary, exacerbated by the dif- ficulties of communicating across time zones.

Your Angel, Dragon, or Vulture may have compromised some of the independence you enjoyed when you first set up, but at least he wasn't your boss. You now have a boss again. Your lock-in period can feel like a jail sentence, but when it comes to an end and the door swings open, you may begin to feel guilty about leaving the remaining members of your team unprotected. What you have built will at best change and at worst be broken up and destroyed. You need to be emotionally prepared for that.

Meanwhile, what about your Angel, Dragon, or Vulture? Will they have escaped scot free once again?

Call me a sentimental fool if you like, but every time a busi- ness I had backed was sold, I felt a sense of regret mixed in with the feeling of success and satisfaction. I knew that in all probability in four or five months' time I would be sharing a melancholy lunch with the CEO and hearing about the diffi- culties the acquirer was causing, and the stream of resignations from the old-timers. Perhaps things would perk up toward the end of the meal when he started talking about the new house in Florida, and airing his ideas about his next venture. All the same, the dominant taste would usually be bittersweet.

But of course, the investors do get away more cleanly than the entrepreneur. For a start, they have other businesses to dis- tract them, to bury themselves in; they do not have to accept the authority of a new boss. And because their involvement in the business is not needed after acquisition, they will not be subject to the aspects of the deal which are designed to tie in the management team. They may lose some upside as a result; quite often the management team will be offered additional equity or other retention incentives which may tip the equity balance in their favor. This in itself has been known to cause suspicion and tension between backer and backed, because equity value is effectively being passed from the one to the other. However, given the extra commitment that is normally asked of the management team in order to get a deal done, some sweetener of this sort is perfectly justified.

The Angel, Dragon, and particularly Vulture will be less likely to be required to give warranties. He will argue that his involvement in the business was non-executive, so that it is not reasonable for him to warrant anything more than that he owns his shares and is free to dispose of them. Sometimes, therefore, this can result in the management team taking a greater warranty burden. If the investors are forced to share in the wider warranties, their liability will probably be limited to an amount placed in escrow. Rightly, no fund manager will ever give warranties which might cause money to be clawed back from his investors, or expose other assets in his funds.

And because the Angel, Dragon, or Vulture's future involvement in the business is not wanted, he may be able to avoid any element of the consideration that is designed to tie the management team into the business for the immediate future. He may be able to negotiate for payments that are deferred to the management team, or performance linked, to be paid to him up front, perhaps subject to a discount. Depending on how things go, of course, that may prove to be either a good or a bad decision.

Sales to financial buyers

In the private equity world, as distinct from venture capital, there have been periods when a high proportion of exits have been delivered by management buy-outs. A business is bought, leveraged with bank debt, and grown or improved a little. The business generates enough cash to pay down some of the debt. Then the original investor sells the business to a new investor for an overall price not very much higher than he paid. Nevertheless, because the leverage has been reduced, he is able to take a tidy profit on his equity. The new investor re-leverages the business, and the process starts again. Successive investors make money by recycling essentially the same asset and achieve their returns through the use of leverage.

This model requires a steady, stable business to make sense and therefore is less often seen in the venture capital world. However, private equity can sometimes provide an exit for venture capital investors if a business has grown to the stage where it is predictable enough for a buy-out structure to work. Quite often private equity houses compete with trade buyers to acquire venture capital businesses. If the business concerned has strategic value to a trade acquirer, and can command a premium price as a result, then it is unlikely that private equity will be able to compete. However, if the value to a trade buyer is less central, the magic of leverage may enable the private equity firm to pay a higher price.

Because of this, it is normal to approach some potential financial buyers as well as trade buyers during the sale process. Selling to a financial buyer has some different dynamics to selling to a trade buyer. For the Angel, Dragon, or Vulture, some aspects of the negotiation may be easier. After all, the buyer is one of them, a member of the same club. But also, because of that, both buyer and seller will want to be sure that they are not embarrassed by later being shown to have done a worse deal than their counterparty. If the buyer goes on to make a monstrous return, the seller will look foolish. If a trade buyer does well out of an acquisition (and more often than not they are disappointed), at least the seller can argue that the price was fair and that the good result came from the buyer's skill in finding commercial synergies and strategic benefits. With a financial buyer that excuse is not available. Embarrassment can turn to real damage if the buyer and the seller share, or want, some of the same limited partners as customers.

For the management team the dynamic is likely to be very different too. In some cases these financial purchases may be structured as management buy-ins, with the new investor installing his own senior management team. In these circumstances it may conceivably be possible for the original entrepreneur to exit faster than would be the norm with a trade buyer. A management buy-out is a more common structure, though, with the existing team obtaining a new backer to take the business further forward, or the amusingly acronymed BIMBO, where some of the old team stay and a new element is introduced from outside.

So at one extreme, this type of transaction is scarcely an exit for you at all. You are likely to be able to take some money "off the table," but if the incoming investor wants you to continue running the business he will not want you to bank too much. In the jargon, he will want to "keep you hungry." How much is too much, and what constitutes keeping you hungry, will vary from instance to instance, but in any event you and your team are likely to have to roll over a portion of your equity into the new deal. You might emerge with a larger stake, or a stake of similar size in a better capitalized business, and some cash in the bank. What is or is not possible will vary from case to case.

Of course, whether this type of transaction suits you better than a trade sale will depend mostly on your preferences. Maybe in your heart of hearts you did want to keep going; maybe you believed your investors were pushing for an exit too early. In that case the new financial buyer, so long as he is someone with whom you can work, may be a very good option. But if you were the one who wanted to exit, clearly this route, which may commit you to another three, four, or five years of slog, may be completely wrong.

As you can see, a clear conflict of interest between you and your existing Vulture has now crept in. He wants the best price he can get. Indeed, he is obliged to try to get the best possible price or he is doing down his customers – his investors – and failing in his fiduciary duty. If a financial buyer offers the best price, but demands that you stay with the business and take very money little out, when you want to exit as soon as possible, what you want and what your Vulture wants may be very different. On the other hand, if you want to stay in and roll the dice again with a new financial backer, but the best offer comes from a trade buyer, the conflict becomes starker still. On occasions I have seen suspicion and bitterness creeping into what should be a positive process, to the extent that the management are sidelined or excluded from negotiations. Openness at an early stage about what everyone is ideally trying to achieve can help to defuse the situation and reach a result which is satisfactory for all parties.

Achieving a trade sale

So that is the destination. Perhaps not quite as described in the brochures, but how do you get there? Part of it, as I said earlier, is about building a good business. It is very difficult to sell a business which is running out of money. Occasionally you find two potential buyers who are keen enough to bid against each other for an interesting piece of intellectual property. In those circumstances a skillful corporate finance adviser may just be able to create enough competitive tension to achieve a vaguely respectable price. Much more often, though, the potential buyer will simply watch and wait while the cash trickles away until he can buy the business for next to nothing just before it goes bust – or buy the assets, leaving the insolvency practitioner to sort out the rest. As usual, get yourself into a position where you have an alternative plan, where you do not have to sell the business but can negotiate from a position of strength.

We hummed and hawed in Chapter 3 about whether to appoint an adviser to help raise that first round of funding. In Chapter 11 we concluded that your existing Vulture or Angel, not an external adviser, should usually lead the fund-raising efforts in the later rounds. Now perhaps I can make it up to my friends in the corporate finance community by stating unequivocally that when it comes to a sale you need an adviser, and you want the very best you can get. Not only can he make the difference between a deal and no deal, but he can also make a very large difference to the price. On exit a good adviser can earn his fees – which when he pitches to you perhaps sound steep, even extortionate – over and over again.

What is more, you should not wait to appoint your adviser until the time has come to sell the business. Good corporate finance advisers can inform the process of preparing a company for sale. If they are good, they should understand intimately the sector on which they focus and make it part of their business to be aware of the characteristics that likely acquirers are seeking. Familiarize yourself with the best advisers well before you want to appoint them; ask them to present to you and your board in good time. Looking ahead will both benefit you and facilitate the job of the firm you eventually appoint.

Clearly, you do not go to your barber shop and ask if you need a hair cut. The answer will invariably be: "Well, yes sir, it does look a little ragged around the edges." No corporate finance adviser will discourage you from selling your business; unless they do IPOs as well, in which case they might see the opportunity for a larger fee down that road. However, a good adviser can be expected to provide sensible advice about timing. They all charge a monthly retainer, but the lion's share of their fee is success based and linked to the size of the ultimate deal. It is therefore in their interests to give you the advice about timing which is most likely to achieve the best outcome.

It is also in their interests to give you good advice about how best to get your company ready for sale, because it makes their job easier. Some of this is simple stuff: making sure that there are no skeletons in the corporate cupboard, no awkward potential lawsuits looming, and that your intellectual property is clearly owned and safely protected. You should make sure that your financial accounts are prepared in a normal way to the right standards, and that you have an auditor of suitable standing. If you are a European or Asian company and expect your likely buyer to be a US corporation, you should make sure that your accounts are compliant with US GAAP, for example, and that there are no technical accounting issues which might damage value on an acquisition.

Other advice might be based on the adviser's past experience of what a particular acquirer might or might not like to see. Some of the issues are obvious. For example, if you have built your product entirely on underlying Microsoft technology then you are less likely to achieve a sale to IBM or Oracle, and vice versa. Nevertheless, a good corporate finance adviser should be able to give you some more subtle insights into what turns individual buyers on and off.

The other advantage of selecting your adviser in good time is that you will be at the forefront of his mind. He will begin to play his part in raising your profile with the companies which might buy you. Sometimes you might even gain commercial benefits in this way. Conversations your corporate financier has with industry majors may initially lead to reseller agreements or other types of partnership.

If your relationship is working well with your Angel, Dragon, or Vulture, he should be able to guide you toward the right advisers. He may have his reasons for pointing you in a particular direction – toward a firm with which he has worked well before, or to which he owes a favor – but that is not necessarily a bad thing. Of course, you should do your own due diligence and make sure that his recommendations make sense. He should also anticipate the corporate finance adviser and give you early advice about how to get ready for a sale. The more attractive you are before talking to advisers, the more likely you are to attract a good one.

Getting bought, not being sold

It goes without saying that ideally you want your company to be bought, rather than having to sell it. The best way to achieve a satisfactory outcome and a good price is to be approached by a purchaser, and then to start a process. It is far less effective to prepare an information memorandum and fire it out to all and sundry in the hope of drumming up interest. You want to create, and help your adviser to create, the impression that you are a sought-after property, that companies are knocking on your door because they want to add you to their corporate portfolio.

Once again, if you have been focusing on building a good business you will have started down this path. In order to be building the right marketing profile with your customers and potential customers, you will already be spending time (and inevitably money) with the key analysts in your industry. This activity will also place you on the radar of competitors – which may be acquirers – and collaborators. Successfully developing channels to market through industry majors can often be a good way of putting yourself on their screen as a potential acquisition target. Often that first approach will come from your closest collaborator. However, you have to be aware (as we touched on when we were discussing the merits of a trade investor in the last chapter) that if you get too close to one partner you might put the others off. It isn't really any different to the school dance or the last-year prom.

IPOS

This section on IPOs has been a long time coming. So it's a bit like an IPO itself. The IPO – the initial public offering, or in European terminology the stock exchange flotation – is often perceived as the pinnacle of success for a venture capital investment.

Why is an IPO better than a trade sale? Indeed, is it?

The perception that an IPO is the ultimate goal is based on a number of things. First of all, the biggest venture-backed successes have culminated in IPOs: Microsoft, Cisco, Apple, Oracle, Intel, Amazon, eBay, Yahoo!, Google, and so on. These examples come to mind partly because the names of those companies continue in the public arena, whereas a company that is bought loses its name and its separate identity and gets obscured by its acquirer, even if it has become a substantial part of the acquirer's business. Fewer people remember Agile, Hyperion, BEA, Peoplesoft, Stellent, Portal, or even Siebel, although without them Oracle would be a far smaller business. Even fewer people will remember those names in the future. Andiamo, Actona, Perfigo, Protego, Sipura, Vihana, Navini, and Nuova may sound like an Italian vocabulary list; in fact they are all the names of largely forgotten multimillion-dollar acquisitions made by Cisco.

Secondly, a really successful IPO creates far more wealth than a trade sale. Often, the majority of this wealth is created after the IPO, not before. When Google went for an IPO at a share price of $85, it was valued at $27 billion. At that stage the stakes of backers Sequoia and Kleiner Perkins were estimated to be worth about $2 billion each, or 160 times their $12.5 million cost. Twelve months later, Google's share price was $285. Sequoia and Kleiner Perkins are estimated to have distributed stock to their limited partners worth $4.5 billion in the course of that year. So more wealth was created for the original investors in the one year after the IPO than in the five years preceding it. At the peak, in December 2007, Google's share price was just under $715, 8.4x the IPO price. Holding the shares to the peak could have turned the venture capital investors' 160x multiple at IPO into about 1,300x.

So that is the pinnacle. Successes of that order are why IPO is viewed as the greatest venture capital peak of all. However, few IPOs are remotely Himalayan in scale. Most are set in far lower mountain ranges. In fact, in many cases foothills might be a better analogy, and treacherous foothills at that.

Just as, at one end of the exit spectrum, the minutiae of different insolvency processes are outside the scope of this book, so at the other is the detail of the IPO process. Different stock exchanges, in different countries, have different rules. The types of business that can float vary from place to place. Some markets cater primarily for larger IPOs, such as NASDAQ; others, such as London's Alternative Investment Market or AIM, cater principally for smaller companies.

However, there are some common characteristics to bear in mind when eying the glory of flotation.

First of all, the IPO itself is likely to be even less of an immediate exit than a trade sale. The majority of shares offered in an IPO are new shares, sold to institutional and sometimes private investors to raise money for the company. In buoyant market conditions, when there is strong demand for a company's stock, some existing shares can be sold. Generally these are a minority of the holdings of the investors, and certainly a minority of the management's. The reasoning here is that investors are buying into the growth story of the newly quoted company when it is likely to be still a relatively young, and quite possibly even unprofitable, business. They are acting almost like later-stage venture capital investors, by providing enough capital to drive the company to success, in the process pushing up the price of their own new shares. The management team, and the pre-IPO investors, are insiders who know the company far better than those buying shares at flotation. If these informed insiders are rushing for the exit when the newcomers are pouring through the entrance, it hardly shows much confidence in the structure of the building. Perhaps it is in danger of collapse, if not now, in a few months' time; or at the very least, the price for which it is being offered looks more like a sell to the insiders than a buy.

Secondly, rather like the secondary private equity investors in a financial exit, the incoming shareholders do not want to see the management team making themselves too cash rich, thereby potentially reducing the motivation they have to make every effort to drive the company forward, and the value of its shares upward. They want the management team's interests to be aligned with their own, and so desire that most of their wealth remains in their shareholding.

It is thus quite possible that on IPO you, your management team, and even your Vulture, Angel, or Dragon are unable to sell any shares at all. Instead, you find yourself required to sign a "lock-up" agreement which prohibits you from selling any shares for at least six months, perhaps twelve months, sometimes even longer. What kind of exit is that?

Well, you might say, at least it's an exit when the lock-up period ends. Then you'll be able to sell your shares. After all, they're publicly listed now. There's a market in them.

Not necessarily. You are insiders. That means that for long periods of the year you cannot trade your shares. This may be within a 30-day period before you announce your results. Some European companies report on a half-yearly cycle, but increasingly the norm is as in the US, with a quarterly cycle. So if you're announcing your results every quarter, the rules of most stock exchanges mean that you cannot sell shares for at least four months out of twelve. In practice, many companies interpret the rules so that share dealing by insiders is prohibited between the end of a financial period and the announcement of the results pertaining to that period. If it takes longer than 30 days to announce the results, which it probably will, especially for the full annual accounts, a larger proportion of the year is out of bounds.

And because you are an insider you may regularly know things about your company which, if known to the market, might affect the price. If your company is working on an acquisition, or a partnership, or an industry alliance, or even a large sale – if any of those might be significant enough to have an impact on the share price and thus to require a public announcement, you will not be able to sell your shares until that announcement is made.

Apart from the legal requirements (which, if breached, can result in criminal charges), it is often difficult for insiders to sell shares. This is because a sale by management is often seen as a lack of faith in the future of the company. If the board are buying shares, that's a good sign. But if they're selling... do they know something we don't? All such insider share trades have to be announced. Some stock exchange rags carefully follow trades by directors and tip the companies where directors are buying, or suggest selling those where the directors are doing the same.

Finally, you have to consider the liquidity constraints of the market on which your shares are quoted. Especially if your company is still relatively small, and your market capitalization relatively low, there is likely to be little trading in your shares. Some days, even some weeks, there might be no trading at all. When there is trading it may be in small volumes: 5,000 shares here worth $8,000, 10,000 shares there worth $16,000. You will not be able to realize your stake, theoretically we hope now worth many millions, by selling it through the market. There is just not enough liquidity, and no prospect of enough liquidity any time soon. You may be worth millions on paper, but it doesn't help to pay for the groceries, let alone that second house you promised the family.

The piles of junk mail that you now receive from charities requesting donations and from private bankers soliciting your business will rub plenty of salt into your wounds.

In order to unlock your newly quantified wealth, you are likely to have to wait until your stockbroker or investment banker judges that the time is right to approach some carefully selected investors with a view to placing some of your shares. Until then, you'd better make sure that your business performs to plan, because if you don't, the share price will tumble, and then you will have to watch your theoretical wealth spiraling downward and come to terms with the receding chance of ever turning any of it into cash.

HIGH ROLLER-COASTER

The investment bank's boardroom table was vast. While some might have questioned the taste of the pale maple with its chamfered edge and dark cherry inlay, none could doubt its opulence. An air of nervous anticipation oozed from the pores of the professionals massed around it. Most nervous of all were the floating company's board, huddled together at one end of the table. They were very conscious, in June 2000, that the tech market had been drifting since March when they had started the process.

The bank's ultra-smooth head of institutional sales was a bit of a showman. He liked to have the whole room hanging on his words. He banged the end of his pile of documents on the polished surface before placing it neatly squared in front of him. Then, impassively, he ran his gaze down one side of the table and back up again. Several people could not meet his eye; two or three of them, including the company's non-executive venture capital directors, twitched nervously.

Then he broke into a smile. "Well, we can confidently price toward the top of the range. 185p, I'd suggest. At that level we would be... let's see..." he paused, entirely for effect, because the all-important number was firmly ingrained in his head, "just over nine times oversubscribed." A sigh of relieved pleasure hissed round the room and several people made as if to talk at once. The head of sales pre-empted them. "And we'll be able to let most of the shoe go – we can place about 10% of the venture investors' holding."

The first venture capital director muttered, "I don't need a calculator to do that sum. 10% of our shares at 10 times the price we paid – that's all our money back in one go." He felt like a hero. He turned to his co-investor with a big grin,

---

scarcely listening to what the investment banker was now saying.

"But we will have to insist on a 12-month lock-up on the rest. That's the clear message back from the institutions – they do not want to see the rest of the VC's stock flooding the market until the company has proved itself. After all, a valuation of 20 times projected sales is quite a big ask."

In his euphoria the lead VC director forgot himself. "I'd just like to thank the bankers for doing such a fantastic job. I am so pleased that I brought the team to you and that we took the decision to run with you. It just goes to show that in difficult markets the best is the best."

A spontaneous round of applause erupted, only the company's chairman looking slightly irritated to have had his thunder stolen.

By the end of the next day the lead VC director was uneasy, however. The share price had closed at a first-day premium of 72%. "Those precious bankers of yours priced it too low, and sold too few of our shares," suggested an envious colleague.

"No way," he said, "you'll see, the price will settle."

But it continued its stratospheric rise. As the company's valuation neared the £700 million mark that would push it into the FTSE 250, tracker funds piled in, driving the price higher still in a thin market. The bankers refused to countenance the venture capitalists' pleas to satisfy some of the market demand by relaxing the lock-up.

Fast forward a few months...

"Surely that's a breach of the Model Code?" The chairman addressed his question to the company's new broker. The bulge-bracket bank had suggested finding a smaller firm when the price plummeted, taking the market capitalization below its minimum client threshold.

"Well, technically, I suppose so. But it's his bankers selling the shares, not him. It would have been helpful if we'd known that he'd hocked them against the loan he raised to invest in his next company. But nobody could have expected the price to fall to the level at which his bank would start selling their collateral to avoid a loss. It'll be OK if we announce it now."

"16p." The lead VC director shook his head in disbelief. "Poor guy. I really feel for him. He must have been worth £40 or £50 million once. After all, he started the whole thing."

His co-investor woefully agreed. "Yeah, but we haven't been able to sell anything either. I wish I hadn't stayed on the board. By the time the lock-up came off the price was in free fall, and there was so much inside information around that there was just no point when we could have sold. Is it really true that somebody wanted to buy the business for $25 million?"

"Yes, that was way back when. A couple of months before we made our first investment, I think."

When, a few months later, the company was sold to one of its competitors for 6p per share, and the venture capitalists still had been unable to sell any of their shares, they probably felt a little less sympathetic about the founder's forced sale at 16p.

BEING A PUBLIC COMPANY

When you became a publicly quoted company you exchanged one form of servitude for another. You may have breathed a sigh of relief when the venture capital Investor Rights or Shareholders' Agreement and all the other tiresome legal documents were consigned to the shredder. Never again would you have to seek your investors' consent to make a $50,000 capital commitment that was not in the annual budget. You might even have danced a discreet little jig when the hated preference stack was consigned to history, and your investors' Series A, Series B, and Series C Preference Shares (the latter those nasty ones with the 2× liquidation preference) were all converted to beautiful plain vanilla ordinary shares of common stock.

However, at least as a private company you made your mistakes in private. If you missed budget it might have provoked a stormy board meeting, and ruffled feathers in Angels' and Vultures' wings. It might have led to failure to trigger bonuses, and maybe even dilution as a result of needing to raise another round. But at least you could overcome those setbacks in private and recover from them.

As a public company you make your mistakes in public. Your new shareholders will understand your business less well that your venture investors did. Listed equity fund managers have much larger portfolios to manage than the busiest Vulture. Each stake they hold is likely to be a far smaller proportion of the whole. And they will generally want to avoid becoming insiders, and suffering the resultant restrictions on their ability to trade the shares, so by definition they are unable to get so far under the skin of the business. Instead, they rely on publicly available information. So if you let them down and underperform in the early days of your life as a public company, they may just dump their shares if they can, or curse you if they cannot while the value of their holding falls to a level at which they lose all interest in it.

And of course, that is not all. Your underperformance is not only visible to your shareholders, it has been splashed all over the newspapers, all over the internet. You may be personally pilloried in the press and on investor bulletin boards. Your failure can be and will be seen by customers, partners, competitors, and your staff.

I remember that the first public company on whose board I sat made the mistake after IPO of proudly stationing in its head office foyer a board showing the daily share price. That was fine when it was going up, but when it started to go down an immovable cloud of gloom settled over the place, which took some time to shift even after the fateful board had been taken away.

Your friends may have felt a frisson of jealousy when they watched your company float. It isn't a good feeling when that jealousy turns to pity. Then, when the first class action appears from a group of aggrieved shareholders – more likely if you have floated in the US than elsewhere – and a whiff of scandal and suspicion taints the air, you may find out that your friends were less close to you than you once thought.

However, before you say to yourself "Well, trade sale it is then," consider the possible rewards if things go right. When things are going well, a public company's higher profile can work strongly in your favor. Staff morale rises. Option holders excitedly watch the climbing share price. Recruitment becomes easier and the quality of unsolicited job applications rises markedly. Customers begin to comment enthusiastically about your strong performance, and competitors turn green eyes at trade shows on your busy stand from the desert of theirs. What is more, you have a strong balance sheet. You can make those investments that you couldn't afford before (so long as they don't have an adverse impact on your quarterly results, of course). You may be able to use your strong balance sheet, or your listed paper, to make one or two strategic acquisitions, to fill gaps in your product range, or to take out a troublesome competitor.

You may have the pleasure of watching your share price steadily rising, increasing your paper wealth, and bringing the day closer when your stockbroker does place a minority of your holding, for more money than you would have made if you'd sold the whole company in a trade sale.

To achieve that, you need to have learned in the private arena the art of managing expectations. The importance of the main lesson of Chapter 8, of setting achievable goals and beating them, is even greater for a public company than a private one. It follows, therefore, that it is unlikely to be sensible to go public until you have a predictable business. If you are still dependent on landing a small number of large and irregular contracts, you are unlikely yet to be a suitable candidate for IPO. If you have a steady stream of repeat revenue from your existing customer base, and if you have been able to adopt a conservative revenue recognition policy so that your CFO has built up a nice reserve for a rainy day in the bottom drawer, then maybe it is right for you.

Just as in a private company, a chairman with relevant experience will be an invaluable ally. In this case relevant experience obviously means having sat on public company boards and having passed through the IPO process already. Some of the rules of public company life are too arcane to cope with unless you've seen them before.

Make sure too that you have board members who understand the public company requirements, but who also understand your business and will be commercial and robust rather than timid and self-concerned when things go wrong. Some or all of your Vulture directors might stay on the board after IPO, although this can be problematic for them because of the way it hampers their ability to sell their shares when the lock-up comes off. If they do have to step down, you might even find yourself missing your Vulture directors. For at some point, something will go wrong. Very few companies maintain an unbroken record of growth, or of achievement against expectations, for more than four or five years. Especially in the technology sector, rapid change militates against an unblemished track record.

The veteran British technology industry analyst Richard Holway gives his "Boring Award" to companies listed on the

London Stock Exchange which have an unbroken record of more than 10 years' growth in earnings per share. Only two companies hold a Holway Boring Award: Sage, known for its accounting software; and Capita, the outsourcing company. They both floated in 1989 and so have maintained their record of unbroken growth for almost two decades. They are the only ones. No other London-listed company in the information technology sector has an unbroken 10-year record.

If you wanted to run a public company for the fun of the game, or to build a really large business to satisfy your ego, then good luck. If it really is more about the money, you might be wise to put an exit plan in place before it's too late, before you stumble and your dream is spoiled. Most smaller public companies get bought by bigger ones, so it may be back to a trade sale once you've used some of your IPO-generated cash to drive some strong growth.

CHAPTER THIRTEEN

The Next One

Will you do it again?

Congratulations on having navigated your way around the Cape of Good Hope. You are relaxing in the warm waters of the Indian Ocean.

Your reputation is unscathed, because most of your investors made the returns they wanted, and the ones who did not (that second round was a bit of a crush) felt that you behaved properly and did what you could to protect their interests.

Your health is strong. The stress-related ailments that became almost too much in the final furlong of the sale negotiations have now settled down. Your ulcer is back under control. Your scabies is soothed by the cortisone cream. Your batteries are recharged, your energy is flowing back. You are even beginning to feel a little bored.

Your bank balance is in great shape. You may not have quite as much as you want, but you definitely have as much as you need.

Your sanity is intact. Well, no actually, because you must have been *un poco loco* in the first place to start off as an entrepreneur. And, just in case any proof is needed, you are thinking of doing it again.

LEARNING FROM EXPERIENCE

Are serial entrepreneurs crazier than their younger selves starting out? In one way yes, because they now know just how much it takes to build a successful business. And in one way no, because they also know how to do it.

I am sure that you have spotted many clichés and misquotes in the course of this book and winced at them. One that many people use, and that always makes me cringe because it doesn't make sense without the line after, is "the world's your oyster." The actual quotation is as follows:

> *Why, then the world's mine oyster,*
> *Which I with sword will open.*

(Shakespeare's *Merry Wives of Windsor*, Act II, Scene II, since you ask.)

Serial entrepreneurs scarcely need a sword. They will be fêted by their first set of backers. They will be wooed by others. They will be presented with oysters that are already open, plump, and juicy. If they want to go around again, and are willing to take in outside investors (for now they possibly have the wherewithal to fund their business entirely themselves, if they so wish), they will find the process shorter and more pleasant than first time around. Investment terms may be markedly more generous.

The most satisfying moments in my venture capital career came when businesspeople who had worked with me once agreed to work with me again. That was the ultimate endorsement, the confirmation that the relationship had been up to the mark. Once or twice I had the embarrassment, and the disappointment, of saying to a team that I had backed before and liked "I'm sorry, I don't think this one will work" or "It doesn't quite fit with our current investment strategy. Can I introduce you to so-and-so down the road?"

In Europe it is often said that there are not enough serial entrepreneurs. Few businesspeople, so the conventional wisdom goes, have the hunger and the ambition to do it more than once. A few million in the bank is enough. The US supposedly contains more people who are hungry enough to do it again, to turn those first few million into a few tens of millions, and then a few hundreds of millions, and then perhaps a few billion. Whether this stereotypical view of the old world and the new is correct, I don't know.

I do know that individuals who have founded businesses and built them to success are very special and that their talents should be reused as many times as possible. I was lucky to learn most of what I know about how to do venture capital with a modicum of success from working with some people like that early in my career. The maelstrom that followed the bursting technology bubble did a great deal of damage to the early-stage investing community. Because of their long track records, the returns they have already delivered, and their exceptional skills, the great top-tier firms – Sequoia, Kleiner Perkins, and the like – have remained relatively unscathed. Success breeds success. However, the emerging promise of many newer firms was destroyed. Many limited partners suffered losses which may have driven them away from this asset class for a long while. Where venture capital once might have attracted talent because of the opportunity to make large sums of money in an activity that is intrinsically interesting, it has become less likely to do so. And the opportunities are fewer.

As a result, the entrepreneurial world is poorer. Mature economies depend on innovation to maintain their vibrancy and to retain a competitive edge. Innovation can dramatically change lives for the better and can help to tackle some of the problems challenging the planet and the human race.

PASSING THE EXPERIENCE ON

I hope that this book has given you a few useful tips that may help you to a successful outcome in your venture. I hope that it will help to place you in a position where you can think about whether or not to do it again, or to consider becoming an Angel, a Dragon, or even a Vulture. Not all entrepreneurs move easily from the active executive role of running a business to the role of investor, but many do become invaluable supporters of the next generation of entrepreneurs. I hope that you might either do it again, or cross over to the dark side, as I did, and lighten it up. Or if not, write a book that gives entrepreneurs even better advice than this one.

Useful Resources

Venture Capital Organizations

❑ NVCA, National Venture Capital Association –
www.nvca.org
❑ EVCA, European Private Equity and Venture Capital
Association – www.evca.eu
❑ BVCA, British Private Equity and Venture Capital
Association – www.bvca.co.uk

These organizations include as members most of the institutional venture capital investors in their geographies. They
publish lists of their members together with their investment
criteria in searchable database form. These data are provided
by the firms themselves and are therefore reasonably accurate,
with the proviso that some firms draw their criteria slightly
wider than reality in order to make sure that they do not miss
good investment opportunities on the edge of their target
areas.

Access to EVCA's list is free. The BVCA's used to be free but
they have obviously fallen on hard times, as they now charge
£150 for database access to non-members and £75 for a hard
copy of the members' handbook. The NVCA charges $195 for
a hard copy and $325 for an annual subscription to their mem-
bers' database. Well, they are venture capitalists, after all.

As well as investors, these organizations include in their
membership advisory firms, corporate finance houses, and
lawyers.

Each organization publishes research about venture capital.
Of course, as they are trade associations, their mission is to
represent the interests of their industry and of the organizations who pay their fees. Read their research with this in mind,
therefore.

They also publish advice for entrepreneurs about how to raise venture capital. While often trade association bland, some of this is not unhelpful.

Both the British and European organizations have "private equity" in their full names but not in their more commonly used acronyms. Am I unduly cynical if I attribute this to the fact that "venture capital," with its early-stage, risk-taking, economically useful image, is the acceptable face of the industry that lobbyists like to turn toward politicians, whereas private equity is a little too much like investment banking?

By not including the region that it represents in its title, one might be forgiven for thinking that the NVCA displays a degree of insularity and arrogance which some feel characterizes some sections of the US industry it represents.

Both the NVCA and EVCA have on their websites a list of worldwide national venture capital associations, which may be useful but which I will not reproduce here. The NVCA also has a list of regional organizations in the US.

There is no umbrella organization covering Asia and other regions, but individual country organizations exist, such as:

❑ Australian Venture Capital Association – www.avcal.com.au
❑ China Venture Capital Association – www.cvca.com.hk
❑ Indian Venture Capital Association – www.indiavc.org
❑ Japan Venture Capital Association – www.jvca.jp
❑ Malaysian Venture Capital Association – www.mvca.org.my
❑ Taiwan Venture Capital Association – www.tvca.org.tw

These are rather more generous than their British and American cousins and provide free lists of their members.

Angel Associations

❏ ACA, Angel Capital Association –
www.angelcapitalassociation.org
❏ BBAA, British Business Angels Association –
www.bbaa.org.uk
❏ EBAN, European Business Angels Network –
www.eban.org

These are the three umbrella organizations for business angel networks in the US, the UK, and Europe. Each provides free links to their members, which in turn offer access to individual Angels in different ways.

Dragons

❏ *Dragons' Den* – www.bbc.co.uk/dragonsden
❏ *Dragons' Den* (Canada) – www.cbc.ca/dragonsden
❏ *Shark Tank* (US version)
– http://abc.go.com/shows/shark-tank

If you dare! To remove temptation, at the time of writing this book, applications for the US show were closed.

Some Industry Publications

❏ *Venture Capital Journal* – www.vcjnews.com. Venture capital in the US
❏ *European Venture Capital Journal* – www.evcj.com. Venture capital in Europe
❏ *Asian Venture Capital Journal* – www.avcj.com. Venture capital (surprise, surprise) in Asia

❑ *Private Equity Europe* – www.privateequityeurope.com. Venture capital and private equity in Europe

❑ *Unquote* – www.unquote.com. Data on venture capital deals in Europe

❑ *Real Deals* – www.realdeals.eu.com. Venture capital deals in Europe

❑ *Prequin* – www.prequin.com. Information on US private equity

❑ *Red Herring* – www.redherring.com. News about private technology companies

❑ *Angel News* – www.angelnews.co.uk. Primarily about angel investing in the UK

❑ *Angels* – www.angelsmagazine.net. For angels and private investors

❑ *The VC* – www.thevc.com. Comic strips for much-needed light relief

Index

Acknowledgments

I would like to thank all the people from whom I learned about the venture capital business: my former colleagues at Quester and the United Bank of Kuwait, the wise Angels with whom I was lucky enough to co-invest, my other co-investors, professional advisers, and most of all the entrepreneurs and management teams with whom I had the privilege to work.

I am very grateful to Robert Dudley, my agent, for encouraging me to embark on this project, and to the excellent team at Nicholas Brealey Publishing for bringing *Angels, Dragons and Vultures* to publication.